# BIRD WATCHING IN
# MALLORCA

Bonelli's Warbler

# BIRD WATCHING IN MALLORCA

BY

## KEN STOBA

CICERONE PRESS
MILNTHORPE CUMBRIA

© Ken Stoba
ISBN 1 85284 053 6

*Front Cover:* Black-winged Stilt

# Contents

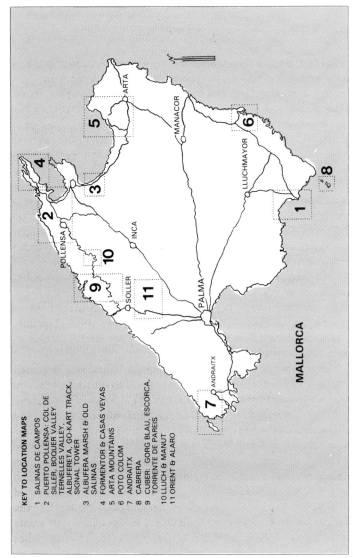

**KEY TO LOCATION MAPS**

1 SALINAS DE CAMPOS
2 PUERTO POLLENSA: COL DE SILLER, BOQUER VALLEY TERNELLES VALLEY, ALBUFERETA, GO-KART TRACK, SIGNAL TOWER
3 ALBUFERA MARSH & OLD SALINAS
4 FORMENTOR & CASAS VEYAS
5 ARTA MOUNTAINS
6 POTO COLOM
7 ANDRAITX
8 CABRERA
9 CUBER: GORG BLAU, ESCORCA, TORRENTE DE PAREIS
10 LLUCH & MANUT
11 ORIENT & ALARO

MALLORCA

# Introduction

It is little wonder that Mallorca is now one of the most popular continental destinations for British birdwatchers, it has so much to offer the visitor who wishes to combine his hobby with a holiday. Most people are unaware of the treasures which lie behind the image presented in the tourist brochures. The vision of miles of concrete discos and hamburger stalls has to be put into its context within the 'real' Mallorca which lies a short distance beyond the ranks of beach parasols. Olive and citrus groves in rich farmland, shaded woodlands, and dusty villages all backdropped by the Northern Sierras whose highest peak is higher than Ben Nevis and whose cliffs plunge vertically into the sea. Of more than 200 miles of coastline less than a fifth is developed; even today there are many areas where the walker can still spend a day without meeting another human being. Many visitors who discover this second face are soon convinced that the scenery is the equal of anywhere in Europe.

The casual visitor may spend a little time finding his or her way around and discovering the best birdwatching sites. Hopefully this book will act as a pointer and will ensure that the maxium time can be spent 'in the field'.

The number of birdwatchers visiting the island has increased dramatically over the past 20 years or so. Many of these newcomers have received their first experiences of birdwatching abroad aided by Eddie Watkinson's *Guide to Birdwatching in Mallorca* and several of the sites covered by that guide are contained in this book. However, since Eddie died in 1980, major changes have taken place. Some areas have been developed and some access restricted: the once famous K8 site on the Pollensa/Soller road no longer holds special interest as the rubbish tip which attracted **Red Kites** has been closed; the fields alongside the track to the Boquer Valley farm are now built over; the 'Toucan Marsh' exists as a shadow of its former self and the path through the Ternelles

Valley is closed more than it is open. On the plus side, the Albufera Marsh is now a Nature Reserve and breeding **Bee-eaters** have returned to the sandworks at Son Boch. This book is an attempt to bring all the information up to date and include 'new' sites which have gained prominence.

British birdwatchers feature high on the list of pioneers for the hobby on the island and I am indebted to those who have gone before for doing most of the hard work. My own experiences on Mallorca have been enriched by the warmth, courtesy and friend-liness of its inhabitants and the many friends I have made during my regular invasions of their island. I have also been fortunate indeed in meeting many of the regular visiting 'birders'. Their willingness to pool information and share their experiences has made me feel like a part of a special club with familar faces turning up at chance meetings. One such occasion took place on the top of Cairngorm and was only slightly marred by the fact that I had been spotted from afar because I was wearing my camouflage coat! I sincerely hope that the users of this book will feel encouraged to join 'the club' and share in the special experience of 'wild' Mallorca which captures and maintains the interest of both beginners and old hands alike.

## Geography and History

Joined at various times to Eurasia and Africa, Mallorca finally separated from mainland Spain around 100 million years ago. The present day island has an area of around 1,400 square miles and extends approximately 55 miles east/west and 40 miles north/south.Spain lies 120 miles to the west and North Africa is 200 miles to the south.

The geology is dominated by the northern mountain chain which also has profound effect on the island's climate. The moun-tains attract cloud and the subsequent rainfall provides water for the abundant vegetation, as well as assisting in the irrigation of the rich alluvial soils on the farmland of the central and south-western plains. None of the water-courses flow throughout the year, so subterranean water is extracted to provide irrigation during the dry months. The mountains also provide shelter from the worst of the winter weather from the continent, creating a much milder and more temperate winter climate than might otherwise be expected. Most rain falls in late autumn and early spring. Winter temperatures in the lowlands rarely reach freezing point and the heat of the summer sun is usually tempered by sea breezes which sustain things around a very pleasant 80°F. The south and west of the island is, overall, warmer and receives less of the rainfall than areas in and around the mountains.

Man first appeared on the scene around 1500 BC, and subsequent changes of management involved the Phoenicians, Greeks, Carthaginians, Romans, Moors, Franks, the Spanish, French and English. Sometime during this rather tumultuous past the effects of farming and charcoal burning resulted in all of the lowland forests disappearing, along with most of the larger mammals, leaving the landscape and habitat in the form in which we find it today.

All the above reasons help to explain why Mallorca is so attractive to birdwatchers, perhaps it should also be mentioned at this point that it is, for the same reasons, a haven for the botanist, entomologist and marine biologist too. Due to geological structure and history, geographical position and climate, a wide variety of habitats are available in a reasonably small area. Where else can one go from vast reedbeds, coastal scrub and woodland, through farmland and arrive 4,000 feet up in the mountains in less than an hour's drive? Finally, climate and geography also combine to produce a habitat unique to Mallorca - the 'Balearic zone' - principally of note for its variety of plants including many endemic species found only there. It exists in those mountain regions immediately below the standard cloudbase and is the result of the combined effects of moisture, altitude and Mediterranean sun.

## Flora and Fauna

It is only possible, in a book primarily about birds, to scratch the surface of the subject of plants and animals and much must be omitted for the sake of brevity. However, it would not be humanly possible to ignore them altogether, as any time spent in the various habitats soon breaks down the resistance of even the most stoical birdwatcher. Distractions abound and some appreciation of the general scene adds spice to the main course. I have also referred to some of the more interesting species in the text of the various locations, where appropriate, and beg forgiveness for such occasional wanderings away from birds.

PLANTS & TREES
Mallorca is a particularly rich hunting-ground for the botanist. For those of us who have a general interest in natural history as well as birds it is quite possible to get engrossed with the plants beneath our feet and not notice the birds at all!

Mention has already been made of the special role which the mountains play as a habitat and it is here that the serious botanist can get to grips with most of the truly endemic plants. The other principal wild habitats are woodland, maquis, garigue and marshland.

**Holm Oak** *(Quercus ilex)* and **Aleppo Pine** *(Pinus halipensis)* are the two main species of trees. The oaks with their shiny, holly-like leaves, occupy the higher ground, extending to the tree-line in the mountains; the pines are widespread throughout the island, particularly noticeable in the coastal dunes.

As for birds, spring is the best time for flowers - although interesting species can be found throughout most of the year. Some, like the magnificent **White Sea-daffodil** *(Pancratium maritimum)* flower late summer and early autumn. The early flowering season covers quite a long period due to differences in altitude: in the warmer, lowland areas plants like the **Asphodel** *(Asphodelus microcarpus)* are well underway in March, yet they bloom as late as June in the mountains.

The most inexperienced botanist will soon notice the introduced **Agave** (century plant) which has naturalised from its original use as a hedging plant. The thick, blue-grey, spear-shaped leaves of this cactus-like plant grow in a rosette standing around 6 feet high and, when the plant flowers (at about 10 years old), it produces an enormous flower spike which towers up to 30 feet from the ground. After flowering the plant then dies, but the dessicated remains of leaves and flower spike remain for some time afterwards.

Plants of marsh, field and wayside are most likely to catch the eye of the casual observer. Those of the farmland range from what seems, at times, to be an unbroken mass of red poppies, to the staggering colours of field edges and verges covered in a bewildering variety of species. The marshes of Albufera and Albuferetta contain large expanses of **Spanish Reeds** which often grow to a height of 18/20 feet and are fringed with stands of tall **Tamarix** and bushes of **Willow.**

The plants which probably attract, if not demand, the most attention are the orchids. The early spring visitor can find a proliferation of these beautiful plants in a variety of habitats. **Bog, Sawfly, Venus, Bumblebee, Pyramidal** and **Bee orchids** head an impressive list of species. When visiting Palma, the tired shopper can break his or her journey by a visit to nearby Belvoir (pron. Beever) Castle where an orchid hunt in the grounds soon relieves the effects of weary feet and an empty purse.

## MAMMALS

None of the large mammals have survived the effects of hunting and habitat reduction. The few species of smaller ones which remain do provide some interest when they pop up from time to time.

The familiar **Brown Rat** and the less familiar **White-toothed Shrew** are common in both towns and in and around the marshes. **Weasels** and **Hedgehogs** may also be seen. Three species of mammal are, perhaps, most worthy of note, and none of them is

11

common by any means. The nocturnal **Genet** *(Genetta genetta)*, which is reported to have a reasonably viable population, is a strange, shy creature. Short-legged with dark brown, blotched buff coat and ringed tail it looks like a cross between a small dog and a cat. (I say looks, but must admit to never having managed to see one myself.) **Pine Martens** *(Martes martes)* are much rarer, my own record being only of one found dead on the Alcudia Puerto Pollensa road and one amazing, broad-daylight sighting of a female taking food to her kittens amongst the rocks of Cuber Reservoir. I cherish this latter sighting as one of the most indelible chance encounters of all my Mallorcan experiences and sincerely hope that the species can maintain its precarious existence. The third species, also with a tenuous foothold as a native, is the 'Gatto Savage' - the genuine **Wild Cat** *(Felis sylvestris)*. Like nearly everywhere else, Mallorca has a large population of feral domestic cats, but their pathetic scragginess does not compare with the heavy, thick-set build of the real wild cat which also has a short, thick, banded tail ending in a blunt tip. Sightings are rare and normally recorded in the more isolated woodlands, but one individual at least hadn't read the book for, on an early morning visit to the Albufuera Marsh, I was amazed to see one swim out of a channel 5 yards in front of me and slowly walk along the path! Even when dripping wet its heavy build was apparent; I was able to watch it for a minute or so until it became aware of my presence and vanished into the reeds on the other side. My meagre store of Mallorquin/Spanish was taxed to the limit when I reported the sighting to the reserve staff as none of them had actually seen one for themselves.

As sightings of these three species are patchy, visitors need a certain amount of luck in seeing them all. I would be interested in hearing any details of casual sightings (see p.89).

This section would not be complete without some reference to bats, which are the most often seen of all the mammals and also notoriously difficult to identify. Around 10 species have been recorded although as a complete bat-novice myself, I can only claim to have seen three of them with any certainty: the **Long-eared Bat** *(Plecotus auritus),* the **Large Mouse-eared Bat** *(Myotis myotis)* and the **Pipistrelle** *(Pipistrellus pipistrellus).*

## REPTILES & AMPHIBIANS

Snakes, lizards, frogs and toads may not be everyone's cup of tea, but several species of them are common and daily sightings of one or more of them can be expected. All species, being cold-blooded, are more active during the warmer days of late spring, high summer and autumn. It is important to note that *none* of the snakes is venomous and they can be observed quite safely at close quarters - providing the subject is willing to sit still, which they usually are not!

Lizards and geckos abound, much to the pleasure of the resident **Hoopoes** which prey on them. The **Wall Gecko** *(Tarentola mauritanica)* can often be seen basking in the sun but is quick to dart away at the first sign of incautious movement. It is generally of fairly uniform brown colour although almost black individuals do occur. The **Disk-fingered Gecko** *(Hemidactylus turcicus)* is more blotchy in appearance and has a barred tail; it is most commonly seen at night clinging to both interior and exterior walls of buildings, preying on the moths which are attracted to the lights. **Wall Lizards** *(Lacerta sp.)* occur mainly in the south of the island and many sub-species exist. The sub-species *L. podarcis lilfordi* is widespread on cabrera and a *Lacerta sp.* can easily be found in the flower beds of the harbour car park of Colonia San Jordi.

Amphibians are represented by the local sub-species of the **Marsh Frog***(Rana ridubanda),* **Green Tree Frog, Green** and **Midwife** toads all of which occur in the damper habitats. **Marsh Frogs** can even be found in and around the water cisterns of the farms.

Three species of snakes are known to occur, with a fourth (the **Ladder Snake** *(Elaphe scalaris)* of doubtful status, although on my last visit I found a young one in the Ternelles Valley. The two commonest, both *Natrix sp.,* are inhabitants of the Abufera and Albuferetta Marshes. The **European Grass-snake** *(N. natrix)* is the largest, females can exceed 6 feet long - which is quite big by any snake standard! Grass-snakes can take exception to being picked up, but the bite is more like a strong grip and the small teeth have difficulty in even drawing blood (I have only twice been bitten by any reptile and both were female grass-snakes), pet gerbils or hamsters can inflict more damage. The smaller but equally common **Viperine Snake** *(N. Maura),* which grows up to 2 feet long, spends most of its time catching small fish when not basking at the sides of the drainage channels. Despite its unfortunate name, which refers to the viper-like zig-zag pattern on its back, it is quite harmless and even passive when handled. The final member of this trio is the nocturnal **Cowl Snake** *(Macroprotodon cucalaris)* which prefers dryer terrain and is rarely seen - one 'strange snake' reported to me from the San Vicente area could have possibly been one of these.

One further denizen of the marshes attracts special attention. The **European Pond Tortoise** *(Emys orbicularis),* which is under threat in a lot of its habitats elsewhere in Europe, is quite common here. It can grow to a foot in length but 9 inches is a good sized specimen. It can be elusive for it is prone to diving into the water when approached, but its dark green carapace dusted with tiny flecks of yellow-green makes it a most attractive creature when seen close-to.

INSECTS
An adequate description of the profusion of the insect life which inhabits Mallorca would fill a substantial bookshelf. In view of this I have restricted myself to a brief outline of those insects which are most likely to attract the attention; namely butterflies, moths and dragonflies.

The magnificent **Swallowtail,** which needs no further description, is common around the marshes where it readily finds its larval foodplant - **Fennel. Wall, Clouded Yellow, Red Admi-**

**ral, Speckled Wood** and **Cleopatra** are also common. Less common species include **Queen of Spain Fritillary, Long-tailed Blue** and **Scarce Swallowtail.**

Of the moths, the **Humming-bird Hawk Moth** is fairly certain to catch the eye. Like miniature humming-birds, seeming at times to be everywhere there is nectar to be found, they zoom about the flowers stopping and hovering to refuel without alighting. The hawk moths are, in the main, nocturnal and several species, like **Convolvulous, Death's Head** and **Spurge Hawk Moth** are reasonably common.

Dragonflies and damselflies are plentiful and spectacular around the marshes. Various 'hawkers' and 'darters' include the impressively large **Blue Emperor Dragonfly** and the slender red *Aeshna squamata*. The glowing claret-coloured *Crocothemis erythraea* can be found sitting on top of the marshside plants looking, from a distance, for all the world like an exotic flower.


## Information and Hints

LANGUAGE
The Spanish or Mallorquin people you meet in resort areas of the island will, more likely than not, be able to speak pretty good English. In the more rural areas the reverse is more often the case. The natural and quite genuine friendliness of the islanders ensures that difficulties are soon sorted out in a combination of sign language and pidgin English/Mallorquin, usually with more than a little mirth on both sides. Students of Spanish should be aware that Mallorquins speak their own brand of Spanish and even spell words differently.


POLITENESS & GREETINGS
The woeful inability of British people to speak, or even attempt to speak, any foreign language is not something we should be proud of. Even the most rudimentary effort to converse in Spanish is very

well received by the locals and a polite 'Buenos dias' ('Good morning'), pronounced locally 'Boo-eh-nah dee-ah,' goes a long way in breaking the ice. Substituting that with 'Buenas tardes' ('Good afternoon/evening' - pron. 'Boo-eh-nass tar-days') or 'Buenas noches' ('Good night' - pron. 'Boo-eh-nass notch-ays') provides a polite greeting for any time of day. The less adventurous 'Hola' ('Oh-la') simply means 'Hello' and is better than nothing. 'Please' and 'Thank you', common courtesies invariably used by any Mallorquin, are 'Por favor' ('Pour fav-or') and 'Gracias' ('Grath-ee-ass') respectively. Any 'Thank you' is usually responded to by 'De nada' ('Dey Nah-dah') which means literally 'It's nothing' in the sense 'You're welcome' or 'Don't mention it'. These seven words or phrases are simple to learn and the way they are received soon encourages a more ambitious approach. A quick resumé follows:-

| | | |
|---|---|---|
| *(Boo-en-nah dee-ah)* | Buenos dias | Good morning |
| *(Boo-eh-nass tar-days)* | Buenas tardes | Good afternoon |
| *(Boo-eh-nass notch-ays)* | Buenas noches | Good evening/night |
| *(Oh-la)* | Hola | Hello |
| *(Pour-fav-or)* | Por favor | Please |
| *(Grath-ee-ass)* | Gracias | Thank you |
| *(Day-nah-dah)* | De nada | It's nothing |

## PRONUNCIATION

The language is fairly easy to pronounce, but while it is mostly 'as read' there are certain differences from English. Vowels are always pronounced individually, a Spaniard reading the English word 'please' for the first time would probably say 'play-a-say' if unaware of the proper pronunciation. The word chocolate is pronounced 'chock-oh-lah-tay' in Spanish.

As Spanish vowels are invariably pronounced the same way, it is quite easy to learn them.

16

HOOPOE

WILLOW WARBLER

| Sounds | English | Spanish |
|--------|---------|---------|
| a - ah | as in cab, pad, mad | Playa - *Plah-yah* (Beach) |
| | | Para - *Pah-rah* (For) |
| e - ay | as in hay, lay, pay | Donde? - *Don-day?* (Where?) |
| | | Tiene? - *Tee-ay-nay?* (Have you any?) |
| i - ee | as in fee, tea, bee | Si - *See* (Yes) |
| | | Mi - *Mee* (Me) |
| o -oh | as in mow, low, sow | Como? - *Coh-moh?* (As/What/ How?) |
| | | Amigo - *Ah-mee-goh* (Friend) |
| u - oo | as in who, sue, too | Mucho - *Mooch-oh* (Much) |
| | | Usted - *Oo-stayed* (You) |

Pronouncing words ending in 'x' or containing 'll' properly can sometimes pose problems for the visitor and a little practice is needed. Try the following:-

Pollo - *Pol-yoh* (Chicken)      Calle - *Cal-yay* (Street)
Mallorca - *Mal-yohr-cah*      Pollensa - *Pol-yayn-sah*
Andraitx - *And-rah-itch*      Mortix - *Mort-eetch*

Where appropriate, I have included some useful words and phrases under the various headings in this section.

## SHOPPING

The resort areas all have a good selection of shops for the tourist to buy gifts, although the days of cheap leather and ceramics seem to be fading fast. Once comparatively expensive, things like films and suntan lotions are more or less on par with prices back home. With films, certain types and speeds are not universally available, so if you have special requirements or prefer a particular make it may be advisable to buy in the U.K. and bring it with you. Mallorca is famous for synthetic pearls which are sold in shops in all the main towns. If a visit to Manacor is on your itinerary, a trip to the factory there is the cheapest way to buy, but gentlemen beware, it is almost impossible to drag the female of the species away!

Shopping for food is easy as local vegetables and meats are all of excellent quality and readily available. Local markets are a must for the avid shopper and supermarkets stock a good variety of all the usual necessities. Good buys include olive oil, (excruciatingly cheap compared to back home), wine, pâté, cheese, fruit and salami-type sausages. Meat, most tinned or frozen goods and dairy produce compare favourably, but coffee and Danish bacon are appreciably dearer.

For those staying in Puerto Pollensa, the supermarket called 'Mir' (100 yards from the harbour on the right-hand side of the Pollensa road) has the biggest selection of goods, including a comprehensive and competitively priced stock of wines, liquors and spirits.

Some shops still close during the middle of the day and it is advisable to enquire locally about half-day opening, Sundays and fiesta days. For banks see - Money.

Words/Phrases

| How much is it/this? | Cuanto es? | *(Quan-to ays)* |
| Have you any ....? | Tiene ....? | *(Tee-ay-nay)* |
| That's all/everything | Todo | *(Toh-doh)* |
| Where is the ....? | Donde esta el (la) ....? | *(Don-day aysta ayl/la)* |
| Chemist | Farmacia | *(Farm-ath-eeah)* |
| Butcher | Carneceria | *(Car-nay-thay-reeah)* |
| Post office | Correos | *(Cor-ay-os)* |
| Supermarket | Supermercado | *(Soopayr-mayr-cah-doh)* |
| Bank | Banco | *(Ban-coh)* |
| Exchange | Cambio | *(Cahm-bee-oh)* |

## MONEY

The peseta is, at the time of writing, hovering around the 200 - £1 mark and convertion calculations are fairly easy to do. Once dealing at or above the 1,000 peseta mark (£5) you should check the current exchange rate more carefully as it can start to make quite a difference.

Money exchanges (cambios) are open nearly all hours but, like hotels, do not offer as good rates as the banks. Banks, however, are only open Monday to Friday 9.00 a.m. - 2. 00 p.m. and Saturday 9.00 a.m. to 1.00 p.m.; they are closed all day Sunday and on fiesta days. I don't know why, but bank cashiers are generally quite surly compared to money exchange staff. Travellers cheques attract a slightly better rate of exchange than cash.

Words/Phrases

| | | | | | | |
|---|---|---|---|---|---|---|
| 0 | Zero | *(Say-roh)* | 20 | Veinte | *(Bay-in-tay)* |
| 1 | Uno | *(Oo-noh)* | 30 | Treinta | *(Tray-in-tah)* |
| 2 | Dos | *(Doss)* | 40 | Cuarenta | *(Qua-rayn-tah)* |
| 3 | Tres | *(Trays)* | 50 | Cincuenta | *(Theenk-oo-ayn-tah)* |
| 4 | Cuatro | *(Quat-roh)* | 60 | Sesenta | *(Says-ayn-tah)* |
| 5 | Cinco | *(Theenk-oh)* | 70 | Setenta | *(Say-tayn-tah)* |
| 6 | Seis | *(Say-ees)* | 80 | Ochenta | *(Otch-ayn-tah)* |
| 7 | Siete | *(See-ay-tay)* | 90 | Noventa | *(Noh-bayn-tah)* |
| 8 | Ocho | *(Otch-oh)* | 100 | Cien | *(Th-ee-ayn)* |
| 9 | Nuevo | *(Noo-ay-voh)* | 2/300 | Dos/Tres-ciente | *(Doss / Trays-th-ee-ayn-tay)* |
| 10 | Diez | *(Dee-ayth)* | 1,000 | Mil (Dos-mil etc.) | (Meel/ Doss-mil etc.) |

## EATING OUT

In a nutshell, eating out in Mallorca is good and cheap. Prices range from a three course bar meal with a glass of wine at about £4 to around £16 (including wine) for five courses in a good class restaurant. Full English breakfast with coffee is £2, or thereabouts. This means that a lot of self-caterers hardly bother with cooking for themselves and dine out most of the time. A handy tip for those on a budget is that if you find a local café or bar with food that suits your palate, it is often possible to negotiate weekly terms with the owner for regular breakfast or dinner at discount rates. Provided that you are happy to eat from the menu of the day (bars serving food are required by law to provide at least one fixed price meal of this type), such arrangements mean that meal times are not as restrictive as they are in hotels. Packed lunches can also be arranged via the same system. Food is almost invariably of good quality, although cooking and quantity can vary so it pays to shop around.

For those based in Puerto Pollensa I can recommend the following:-

**Pepe's,** a bar/restaurant conveniently situated near the Boquer Valley in Cale Mendes Nunez (off the Formentor road, three roads towards town from the path), at the Alcudia end of the seafront near Motos Formentor. Good cheap food - especially breakfast which is less than £2, including coffee. Pepe, the owner, likes English people and is getting used to birdwatchers, and their requests for 'breakfast' well past noon! He will arrange special rates for regular business.

**Restaurante El Cano,** in the town centre off south side of the Pollensa road. First class food. Swiss owned. Prices on the upper end of the scale, but has an excellent menu of continental haute cuisine.

**Ca'n Pacienci,** set back 50 yards from the north side of the Pollensa road near Pollensa town itself. Probably my favourite. Fixed price extensive five course menu around £20, includes half bottle of excellent house wine. Staff are a delight. Booking essential, even in off-peak season, telephone 530787.

**Goleta,** on the seafront 200 yards towards Alcudia from the marina roundabout. Good food, well served. Varied menu includes local dishes, £4-£7 including wine.

**Rosa Blanca,** a bar/restaurant half a mile outside town on the south side of the Pollensa road. English-type pub food at reasonable prices. Swimming pool for patrons.

## DRINKS

### Words/Phrases

| | | |
|---|---|---|
| Beer | Cerveza | *(Thayr-vay-thah)* |
| Red Wine | Vino Tinto | *(Bvee-noh teen-toh)* |
| White Wine | Vino Blanco | *(Bvee-noh blan-koh)* |
| Rosé | Rosado | *(Roh-sah-doh)* |
| Sweet | Dulce | *(Dull-thay)* |
| Dry | Seco | (Say-koh) |
| Lemonade | Limonada | *(Lee-mohn-ah-dah)* |
| Mineral | Mineral | *(Mee-nay-rahl)* |
| Coffee/Tea | Cafe/Te | *(Cah-fah) (Tay)* |
| -"-/-"- with milk | con leche | *(Cohn lay-chay)* |

### FOOD

| | | |
|---|---|---|
| Steak | Bistec | *(Bee-stayk)* |
| Pork | Cerdo | *(Thayr-doh)* |
| Fish | Pescado | *(Pays-cah-doh)* |
| Bread | Pan | *(Pahn)* |
| Cheese | Queso | *(Kay-soh)* |
| Pâté | Pate | *(Pah-tay)* |

## COMPLAINTS

It is compulsory for all businesses to have a supply of complaint forms for use by dissatisfied clients. They are called 'Oja de reclamaciones' *(oh-ha day ray-clam-ass-ee-ohnays)* and must be provided on request. They are a useful last resort in cases of serious complaint, when failing to get satisfaction on the spot. The business is liable to be fined or even closed if a sufficient number of complaints are received by the authorities, so most complaints are dealt with before things get that far.

## PACKAGE DEALS & SPECIALIST BIRDWATCHING HOLIDAYS

Many companies run package deal holidays and the preferred resort for birdwatchers - Puerto Pollensa - now features in several brochures. Choices in this area can be quite limited as the resort is a minor one in the eyes of most companies and early booking is advised. I would strongly recommend either a self-catering or bed and breakfast deal because, due to little competition, the food in the hotels can be monotonous and generally does not compare with that in bars and restaurants. I say that this is generally the case but, doubtless, there are many good hotels - my opinions are purely personal.

Although most companies offer a limited choice, except for during the high season, good accommodation is not difficult to find. The more adventurous visitor might like to try a 'flight only' trip and make his/her own arrangements.

The small resort of Cala San Vincent does not have quite the same facilities as Puerto Pollensa, but it makes a suitable alternative. It is set in a very scenic but more isolated setting and a car is necessary to get around.

There are quite a lot of specialist companies running birdwatching holidays to Mallorca and, whilst it is quite an expensive way to do things, they do provide a comprehensive package and give good service. One word of caution if you are considering one, first find out how experienced the leader is with the locality. It may seem remarkable, but I know of at least one occasion when the official guide had never visited the island before! It is even more remarkable as the company involved turned out to be one of the better known names in the business.

## WHAT TO TAKE WITH YOU

| | |
|---|---|
| Waterproofs | It can and does rain, particularly in spring and autumn, so these are essential. |
| Footwear | I find that lightweight training shoes are best for general use; something stouter is useful for in clement weather. |
| Long trousers | Walking through scrub is not recommended in skirts or shorts, trousers minimise insect bites. |
| Insect repellent | Mosquitos are no bigger a problem than else where, but they particularly frequent the marshes. I prefer one of the stick-type re-pellents (Autan is the most effective, it's not sticky and has a pleasant citrus smell). |
| Film | Standard types are available, but if you prefer a particular brand of A.S.A./iso, is is better to take a supply. There is a specialist camera shop in Pollensa town, just off the main square. |
| Driving Licence | Officially you require an international driving licence (available from the R.A.C. or A.A.) to hire a car. In practice the standard U.K. licence is accepted. |
| Medicines | Medicines and pharmaceutical goods are ex-pensive, so it is advisable to take all you need with you.Don't forget to take a small selection of antiseptic cream, bandages and plasters to deal with the odd bump and scratch. |

**Note**: The water in Mallorca is perfectly safe to drink, but a change of climate and/or water can effect your stomach so a supply of suitable medicine comes in handy. Also during hot weather, the body loses a lot of salt from perspiration - salt tablets prevent this becoming a problem.

Finally, don't forget the camera, binoculars and telescope!

## POLICE, CRIME & THE LAW

The police force is split into three broad sectors. First, the Guardia Civil - armed police in green, military-style uniforms with distinctively shaped shiny headgear. They are responsible for dealing with all serious crime and are part of a national force. Second, local police - employed by the various municipal authorities, they handle minor offences, parking and traffic control. Their uniforms vary from place to place. Thirdly, traffic police - mounted on motor cycles and always in pairs, they are responsible for traffic control outside the main towns.

The police do a good job and are respected within the community. Laws are enforced and visitors are strongly advised never to suggest that being foreign allows them special privileges. If you should transgress, a polite, attentive attitude is by far the most likely way to turn a ticket into a caution. The police themselves are polite and you, in turn, can be so by addressing them as 'Senor ' *Sayn-yohr* ('Sir'). Considering what they have to put up with at times, they are remarkably tolerant of erring visitors.

Crime is not rampant on Mallorca, but thefts from vehicles are common and pickpockets and hand-bag snatchers also take their toll, particularly in and around Palma. A few simple precautions can be taken:-

Never carry more money than you need.

Leave valuables, travellers cheques and passports in the hotel safe or locked in your apartment.

Do not change travellers cheques into cash until required.

Do not leave *anything* (even towels or sunglasses) exposed inside a vehicle. Leave unnecessary items at home and lock the rest in the boot.

Do not leave valuables unattended on the beach.

The general rule of law applies much as it does in the U.K. and you are unlikely to fall foul of it if you conduct yourself as you are expected to back home. One small point to remember is that you should not take photographs of military installations unless you want a long holiday at the expense of the Spanish government! A few of the particular laws relating to motor vehicles are detailed in the section on cars and car hire.

## CARS & CAR HIRE

Having the use of a car for at least part of your holiday allows you to travel freely between all the places contained in this book and gives flexibility when changing plans to suit the weather. It also allows visits to places like the Arta Mountains which are not accessible by public transport.

Taking a car to the island is expensive and involves a long drive and a ferry crossing, so most people prefer to hire. Hiring a car is both cheap and easy, although prior booking is advised from June to September.

The international companies which have offices at the airport are convenient, but they tend to cost more than most of the local firms which will also provide vehicles for collection at the airport. Insurance is arranged with the hire and it is advisable to take out collision damage waiver (C.D.W.) which covers accidental damage to the vehicle. All persons who may drive must be mentioned on the insurance document. I have never had any trouble hiring a vehicle using a standard U.K. licence but, officially, you should produce an international driving licence. This is a copy of the details of your licence with foreign language translations and is available through the A.A. or R.A.C..

If you are staying in the north of the island I can recommend **Motos Formentor,** situated on the coast road at Puerto Pollensa, a short distance south of the marina's car park. R.S.P.B. members get a discount when booking direct here, the vehicles are reliable and the service is friendly. The phone number is 531 492 (from Britain dial 010-3471 first). If you give your flight arrival time they will deliver a car to the airport and leave a key for collection from the car park attendant. Alternatively, if transfers to and from the airport are included in your package, they will arrange delivery to your holiday address or you can collect from their offices.

**Note:** If you are collecting from the airport, please remember to have some Spanish currency to pay for the car park fee (50p-£5 depending on the time between delivery and your arrival).

## MOTORING LAWS

In the main, the motoring laws are similar to those we are used to. The following are differences where particular attention is needed:-

1. The Spanish drive mainly on the *right,* it saves a lot of trouble if you do too!
2. Dipping of headlights to both approaching vehicles and vehicles in front of you is obligatory. Fixed penalty tickets are issued as reminders to those who don't
3. Seatbelts must be worn by the driver and all front seat passengers outside built-up areas. Small children should not be carried in the front seat.
4. Indicators must be used when overtaking anything, even a bike.
5. Parking restrictions apply where there are red and white squares on the kerbside. Also, you should not park within 3 metres of a corner or on *any* road outside a built-up area.
6. Always park facing the same way as the flow of traffic, *never* on the wrong side of the road.
7. Zebra crossings: we allow pedestrians precedence, Mallorquin motorists ignore them. Moral - pedestrians beware!
8. 'Give Way' and 'Stop' signs must be, and are, observed. 'Give Way' in Spanish is written 'Ceda el Paso', 'Stop' is 'Stop'.
9. Spare bulbs must be carried as it is an offence to have a defective light and no spare. If you are in a hire car, the company will pay the fine - it's cheaper than replacing 'borrowed' sets of bulbs!

## BIRDWATCHERS

With a couple of notable exceptions (laws of libel permitting only passing mention), the local Mallorquins are amazingly tolerant of - and even friendly to - birdwatchers. In spring, when the bulk of the 'migrant' birdwatchers arrive, most of the habitats hold examples of the various species; 'birdwatchers', 'birders', 'twitchers', 'dudes', 'stringers' and 'normal humans'. That there is little conflict between local and immigrant is down to two things; firstly that the birdwatchers are well behaved, and secondly that the locals are very courteous to strangers. In the interests of maintaining this 'bonhomie' the following guidelines should be observed.

Access to land is probably less restricted than it is in the U.K.. Fences and walls are erected for a purpose and should be respected. Paths leading to the sea are all public rights of way (see p.37 Ternelles Valley). Public footpaths are signposted with a silhouette symbol. Other paths not clearly signposted 'Entrado Privado' or 'Camino Privado/Particular' are usually across private land and can be used with discretion, taking care to keep to the path, not walking on crops and not finishing up in someone's backyard. If you greet anyone you meet with a polite 'Hola' or 'Buenas dias/tardes' you are sure to be treated politely and, if you are somewhere you shouldn't be, apologetically given directions to where you can go instead. You can explain your presence by saying 'Miro los pajeros' ('Mee-roh los pah-hay-rohs') - 'I am watching the birds'. Common sense tells you where you are not likely to be welcome and I have never personally been asked to leave. I have, however, on several occasions been treated to a guided tour of the 'estate' of which the owner is very proud and pleased to show off to an interested 'guest'. While this can distract from birdwatching, it does go a long way in cementing good relations.

Photography is, again, not a problem. With the exception of military establishments and personnel, there are no restrictions. When photographing people you should make it obvious what you are doing and ask their consent. The only problem then is to get them to carry on normally and not have them all wanting to get in on the act.

Photographers have the need to approach their subjects quite closely, even when using big lenses. Other birdwatchers should try to give them some consideration and as wide a berth as possible. On one occasion, my hide was visited at 15 minute intervals by a procession of people who stood alongside it or even in front of it to see what was going on. Some even lifted the flap to see who was at home! Even when 'rough shooting' it can be quite galling to have stalked a bird for half an hour and have someone walk over and say 'got any good shots?' Photographers themselves have to consider both the birds and other people. Nest photography is not recommended, it does disturb the birds and the restrictions of a short holiday mean that even the expert hasn't time to aclimatise his subject to his presence. It is far better to observe the birds and ascertain favourite perching sites away from the nest. Also remember that the urge to make a closer approach must always be tempered by the presence of other people - they won't appreciate it if you move forward and disturb something they wanted to watch.

When all is said and done, practically without exception, I have found the birdwatchers I have met on the island tend to respect each other, the island's people and its wildlife. Some are regulars, but even the first-timers find that they all form a sort of club, recognising fellow sufferers and exchanging knowledge and information (see reference to bird meetings and species list under Puerto Pollensa).

Spotted Redshank

# Puerto Pollensa

LOCATION
North-east coast, 8 kilometres north of Alcudia.

ACCESS (See Map p.30)

**Boquer**

From Puerto Pollensa harbour take the Formentor turn-off at the roundabout and turn right almost immediately to follow the Formentor road. The route to the Boquer starts between the new apartments opposite the Avenida Bocharis (which is the sixth road on the right). Vehicles can turn left here at the green and white 'Supermarket' sign to park off the main road. The path, which is a public right of way, leads through the farmyard and into the valley via a gate in the yard.

**Bar Tropicana Track**

Along the minor road signposted 'Bar' and situated, from Puerto Pollensa on the left-hand side of the Puerto Pollensa/Pollensa road about half a mile past the Rosa Blanca, a bar/restaurant.

**Postage Stamp Wood** (See text under Boquer)

HABITAT

Citrus and olive groves leading through farm and garden to maquis-lined valley with a small pinewood. The whole valley is bordered by steep crags, terminating in a small beach surrounded by sea cliffs.

BIRDS

**Boquer**

The Boquer is one of the best known of all the bird haunts on the island and is ideally situated for those staying in Puerto Pollensa and it is only a short walk from the town centre. Running north-

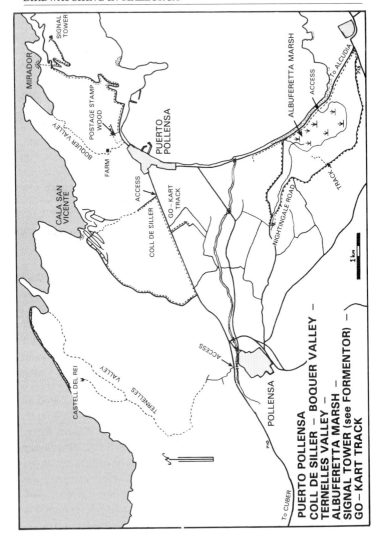

**PUERTO POLLENSA**
**COLL DE SILLER – BOQUER VALLEY –**
**TERNELLES VALLEY –**
**ALBUFERETTA MARSH –**
**SIGNAL TOWER (see FORMENTOR) –**
**GO – KART TRACK**

east/south-west, it provides shelter for tired migrants when the wind is north to north-east. At times of adverse weather in early spring, the valley may be carpeted with birds which are being held back. At other times it is a natural route for north-bound migrants to take and a constant trickle of birds heads through. The first part of the route from the Formentor road to the farm used to be rough fields, good for migrants, but is now developed for apartments. The first point of interest is the olive grove in the bend in the track where migrating **Wrynecks, Pied Flycatchers** and many different **Warblers** can usually be found. I have seen as many as seven wrynecks in one olive tree here! The area of scrub on the right, around the bend, often pays dividends as it favours the odd **Melodious** or **Icterine Warbler** which may turn up. At the near end of this scrub is a small area containing a patch of prickly pear cactus in and around which I have had close views of **Marmora's Warblers** which are more often thought to frequent the maquis further into the valley.

The garden of the farm usually has a pair of resident **Cirl Buntings,** as well as **Marsh Frogs** in the small pool-like water cistern. At the farm itself, the low wall on the left provides an excellent vantage point from which to overlook the farmland and the apricot tree, immediately below the wall, seems to attract a huge variety of migrants almost within touching distance. A little time spent here can usually be quite rewarding as birds, particularly warblers, come into the tree from the left and spend a minute or two before heading off to the right. It seems remarkable that they should all conform to this pattern, but I can vouch for it particularly since having seen a **Wood-warbler, Willow Warbler, Bonnelli's Warbler, Sub-alpine Warbler** and a **Blackcap** all do it within the space of half an hour! Around 11.00 a.m. seems to be the best time for **Raptors,** moving north-east along the mountain chain, and the vista from the farm wall makes a good vantage point from which to see them. With a good telescope it is even possible to see **Black Vultures** around the summit of Tomir, 17 kilometres to the west.

Reluctantly leaving the farm behind, the path through the gate leads us into the valley proper, but it is not until passing between the two large rocks that the scene extends before us. **Blue Rock Thrushes** are common on the crags and these large rocks are often perches for singing males. The high, and at times indistinct path some 100 yards to the right parallels the main path which conforms more strictly to the valley bottom. The crags on the left hold breeding **Ravens** and usually one pair of **Peregrine Falcons** in the spring, but in the autumn they are a stronghold for **Eleonoras Falcons** which breed there in large numbers. I have received reports that a pair of **Egyptian Vultures** bred in the valley in 1988 (confirmed breeding in 1989) and at least one bird has been present there for the last few years. The small pine wood a short way along the valley generally produces something in the way of **Firecrests, Serins** and a **Warbler** or two. Unless the weather is such as to produce a 'fall' of migrants, it is a suitable point to consider retracing one's steps as (if I dare say it) the best has usually been seen. Those wishing to continue may find **Red-legged Partridge** near the end of the valley and take a refreshing swim off the small beach - it can be quite a slog on a warm day. Sometimes there are large rafts of **Ballearic** and **Cory's Shearwaters** off the point, but these are usually a fair distance out and are more easily seen elsewhere. Returning through the scrub along the higher path, a search should be made for **Wrens,** which are a bit thin on the ground on Mallorca, or even a **Marmora's Warbler. Sardinian Warblers,** of course, abound.

## Postage Stamp Wood

It time permits, when reaching the road again, turn left towards Formentor for about 200 yards and enter the small wood on the left. It is surprisingly rich in birdlife with resident **Spanish Crossbills** and **Firecrests,** as well as the associated garigue which ensures a diversity of habitat for **Blackcaps** and **Garden Warblers.** The loud 'Weeel-eo' calls of migrant **Golden Orioles** may also be heard, but they can be surprisingly difficult to locate

CIRL BUNTING

AVOCET

GRIFFON VULTURE
WOOD WARBLER

GLOSSY IBIS

in such cover. On emerging from the far side of the wood you come across a wide expanse of tarmac road, which seems to be far wider than necessary and rather out of place. This part of the new by-pass has been christened 'the runway' and, so far, only leads down to Albercutx (pron. *Al-bayr-cootch*) Farm. The farm was once a very popular haunt for birdwatchers but the gates are now locked and you are not welcome. 'The runway' does allow some access to the scrub near the farm and a walk along here and a peek over the wall can be worthwhile. Calm days may bring **Marmora's Warblers** out of hiding in the scrub. Whilst not recommending it in preference to the Boquer, the area does have its own merits and it is well worth spending some time there. Another advantage is its proximity to the beach cafés and bars which allow the thirsty birdwatcher refreshment whilst listening to the **Serins** in the trees or maybe even watching an **Osprey** fishing in the bay.

## Bar Tropicana Track

Once known as the Go Cart Track and easily located by the 'Go Carting' sign at the end of the road. The sign has now gone, as have, apparently, the **Rock Sparrows** which were the local speciality. This short stretch of road leads past a small wood, an orchard and citrus groves. The area beneath the fruit trees is cultivated with various different migrants. **Wagtails** and **Wheatears** if the ground is newly planted and **Warblers** when the fields are in full growth. The trees themselves also attract birds and on a good day, when there are plenty of migrants around, what started off as a quick visit before going on to one of the other sites on the island, can delay things until well after lunch! **Bonelli's Warblers** take a bit of sorting out from the more common **Willow Warblers** and **Chiff-chaffs,** but they do occur regularly. **Black-eared Wheatears** like the more open ground and once I was treated to a text-book illustration here when I saw one with a pale-form bird standing immediately behind it - both birds were in full profile just like in the field-guides! As mentioned above, the **Rock Sparrows,** which used to be regularly reported from here seem to be in short supply nowadays, but there are still the odd sightings from nearby locations like Coll de Siller (see p.35).

## GENERAL

Puerto Pollensa is *the* resort for birdwatchers as it gives easy access to most of the noteworthy habitats. Quieter and more refined than Alcudia, it still has plenty to offer in the way of excellent bars and restaurants whilst retaining a little of its own character and charm. It is also a popular spot for the local Mallorquins to visit on their days off.

.For visitors who are self-catering the local market, held on a Wednesday between 7.00 a.m. and 12.30 p.m., is excellent for stocking up on local produce.

## BIRD MEETINGS

The Hotel Pollentia, situated on the seafront 400 yards south of the harbour car park is where, each Monday and Friday from the first Monday in April, or Easter if it is earlier, up to and including the second week of May at 9.00p.m. visiting birdwatchers meet informally to exchange information. The meetings are also held in Autumn during the last two weeks of September and the first two weeks of October. A bird list is now also kept on the notice board at Rosa Blanca, a bar quarter of a mile from town on the Pollensa road, and bird watchers are welcome to call in to read and record information. Anyone wishing to make contact and meet other bird watchers may call in at 8.30p.m. any night during April and May. Visitors can help this concession to continue by buying a drink at the bar.

# Coll de Siller

LOCATION
North-east between Puerto Pollensa and Cala San Vicente.

ACCESS (See map p.30)
On foot, via the minor road opposite the Rosa Blanca (a bar on the Puerto Pollensa/Pollensa road), through woods to follow wall on the left over the low saddle in the mountain ridge and down the hill to San Vicente.

HABITAT
Pinewoods, scrub, rock slopes.

BIRDS
On the trail of the elusive **Rock Sparrow** again. The walk along the road and over the ridge - a not too difficult climb of just over 200 feet - may bring success. Don't neglect the road up to the woods as they have been seen on the telephone wires here! Even if the sparrows aren't co-operative the walk is around 2 miles each way with bars at each end. **Blue Rock Thrushes** are common on the crags and migrant **Raptors** including **Honey Buzzards** may be seen along the way. On reaching San Vicente the woods on the left at the far side of the main road abound with **Firecrests; Willow** and **Wood Warblers** pass through the trees beneath which **Sawfly** and the strange, leafless, parasitic **Orchid** *(L. abortivum)* occur.

The more active visitor may like to return from San Vicente along the Pollensa road through the valley and thence back along the main Puerto Pollensa road to the starting point (about 5 miles). The road from San Vicente to the main road is level and bordered by woods, arable farmland and citrus orchards which always produce an interesting crop of birds, Resident **Hoopoes** and **Cirl Buntings** are often sharing the same fields as **Wrynecks**, **Bee-eaters**, **Golden Orioles** and **Nightingales**. The effort in making the walk is certainly unlikely to be wasted, while a bus or taxi for the 2 miles back along the main road saves ears sensitive to traffic!

Spotted Flycatcher

# Ternelles Valley

LOCATION
North-east, near Pollensa town.

ACCESS (See map p.30)
Access used to be by permit only. Permits are issued by Banco son March which is situated in the main square of Pollensa Town - Mondays only before 10.00 a.m. and valid on day of issue only. At present the path is open on Saturdays from 9.00 a.m. and visitors are logged in and out. However, details have varied widely in the past and should be checked as there is no guarantee that they will not change again.

The road to Ternelles is signposted opposite the Roman bridge on the edge of the town, on the Soller road near the main junction of the Palma/Pollensa and Puerto Pollensa roads. Limited parking is available near to the gates of the March Estate through which the path runs, there is no vehicular access beyond this point.

HABITAT
River valley, farmland, crags, pine and oak woods leading to sea cliffs.

BIRDS
In spring, the small river provides moisture among the shade of the trees making the lower valley one of the most pleasant walks on the island. **Robins** and **Dunnocks** are primarily winter visitors, the former is common but strangely unconfiding, whilst records of the latter are probably under-recorded. I have one personal record of **Short-toed Treecreeper** from here in suitable enough habitat to warrant future attention. Migrating **Raptors**, such as **Honey Buzzards** pass overhead, often attended by

the resident **Peregrines**. **Wrynecks** and **Nightingales** hide in the greenery, more often to be located by sound rather than sight and, after the main passage, some remain to breed.

The open fields of the farmland are good for **Wagtails**, **Pipits** and **Woodchat Shrikes** which habitually perch on the fenceposts and sprinklerheads. On passing through the next gate, the path leads on through oak woods attractive to **Redstarts**, **Pied** and **Collared Flycatchers**, **Wood** and **Willow Warblers**. These give way to pines and a chance to see the resident **Firecrests** and **Spanish Crossbills**. Through the pines, into more open country, the path branches, with the left-hand path leading upwards to the castle. The valley is a prime spot for **Black Vultures** which sometimes arrive in small groups of three or four, and in 1989 three **Egyptian Vultures** turned up together. It was near this branch in the track one day that I came across four B.V.s feeding on a sheep carcass - an unusual sight because they are very rarely seen feeding (it is far more usual to see them in flight or resting on one of the many crags). The scrub gives way to rocky slopes with tussocks of grass as the path finally reaches the castle. Lunch, surrounded by the open vista of the mountain top, is usually spent watching **Ravens** and **Rock Doves,** and passing raptors and migrants like **Wheatears** and **Hirundines**. Returning the same way is mainly downhill, with the chance to pick up any species missed on the way. Time for a more leisurely browse through the more interesting flora of both mountain top and riverside. The endemic forms of **Hypericum** and **Cyclamen** both grow alongside the path and **Hares** may also be seen (some friends and I came close to a hare on the path which we were convinced was a blue hare which, to the best of my knowledge, is not supposed to occur in the Ballearics).

GENERAL
Although a public right of way to the sea, right of access to the valley is being disputed by the owners and conditions could change from the details given above. There has been trouble with people

lighting fires.

If you are intending to go all the way to the Castell del Rei it is advisable to start the 2.5 hour walk as early as possible to avoid having to make the last steep part of the walk during the hotter time of the day. Whilst not likely to produce more in the way of birds, the effort is well worth it as the views are spectacular. Remember to take plenty to drink.

# Formentor and Casas Veyas

LOCATION
North-east of island.

ACCESS (See map p.41)
From Puerto Pollensa/Pollensa road, 150 yards from Puerto Pollensa seafront, follow minor road signposted Formentor. The road runs right along the peninsula for 15 milometres/9.5 miles to Cabo Formentor. Casas Veyas is situated 2.5 kilometres/1.5 miles past the left turn signposted Cabo Formentor/Faro.

HABITAT
The road passes through very variable terrain; maquis, garigue, oak and pine woodland, crags, scree, sea cliffs and farmland all feature in this area which is now a National Park. The coastal views are particulary beautiful.

BIRDS
The road climbs rapidly from behind the Albercutx Farm, via a series of hairpin bends to the car park at the Mirador Viewpoint where there is a monument to the engineer Antoni Coll, who built the road over the spectacular crags of the peninsula. The scrub is full of **Sardinian Warblers** and is favoured by migrant **Wheatears** which often seem to appear on almost every prominent rock. Arriving in the very early morning, when the sea mist curls around the cliffs, you may hear a strange, surprisingly loud scything noise which cuts the silence. This is the sound of the air rushing through the wings of the resident **Rock Doves** as they plummet over the edge of the cliffs to swoop into the rock clefts which shelter their nests; speed is essential as they are a favoured prey of the **Peregrine Falcons** which also breed in the area.

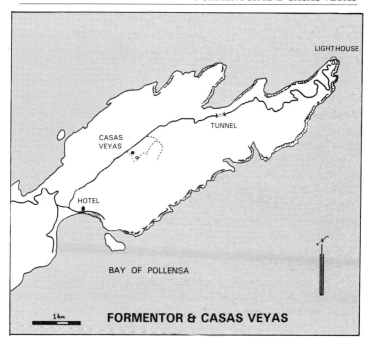

LIGHTHOUSE

CASAS
VEYAS

TUNNEL

HOTEL

BAY OF POLLENSA

1 km

**FORMENTOR & CASAS VEYAS**

The road which climbs out of sight opposite the car park leads to the old signal tower on top of the crag. This road is now open to traffic and stops just short of the tower itself. Gone are the days when the intrepid birder had to footslog all the way to the top under a load of cameras and telescopes. The tower, part of a coastal chain built to give prior warning of invaders from the sea, affords an excellent vantage point from which to observe migrant raptors. An hour or so spent here around 10/11.00 a.m. can be exceptionally fruitful, as depending on the cloudbase,* the birds pass at almost eye-level. Whilst not having the quantities expected at the likes of Gibraltar, the number of species can often compete. **Common** and **Honey Buzzards**; **Red** and **Black Kites; Marsh, Hen** and **Montagus Harriers,** and if you're lucky a **Hobby** or **Short-toed Eagle.** As Casas Veyas is a good place for lunch, I usually backtrack to the main road and turn right to continue toward the Cabo.

**Casa Veyas**
Shortly after the left turn to Cabo Formentor, the road emerges from the woods for a short distance and there are low stone walls on either side. This is the farm at Casa Veyas and vehicles can be parked in the shade of the trees on either side of the gap. The fields on either side of these walls can be a remarkable place for migrants, the high field on the left often holds a completely different variety of birds from the lower field on the right.

One day the field margins may abound with male **Pied Flycatchers** to be followed, a few days later, by migrating females when hardly a male is in sight. **Redstarts** flit between the fig trees, which attract many other species like passing **Bee-eaters, Golden Orioles** and **Warblers** by the dozen. The ground below the trees can be a kaleidoscope of constantly changing passerines, too many to detail. I have seen as many as 200 **Wagtails** in a group including **White, Yellow, Blue-headed** and **Ashy-headed** all

---

*When the clouds are low they bring the raptors lower, but there is little point in visiting the tower when it is shrouded in cloud and visibility is reducted to a few yards.

working their way slowly across the open ground. The impressively long tailed **Rufus Bush-robin** has turned up on a couple of occasions and **Ortolan Buntings** may put in an appearance. Don't forget the skies above. Sometimes it can be difficult to know whether to look up or down as the clear space around the farm affords a good view of the surrounding mountain ridges along which the migrant raptors move. On one visit a **Sparrow-hawk** (a rarity), **Black Kite, Honey Buzzard, Black Vulture, Hen-harrier, Marsh-harrier, Booted Eagle** (resident), **Peregrine Falcon** (resident), **Eleonoras Falcon** and **Kestrel** (resident) all passed in the space of 2 hours without my having walked more than 200 yards.

On the rare occasion when things appear a bit quiet, a return visit on the way back from the lighthouse at Cabo Formentor can be worthwhile as a new batch of different species has often arrived. I always do this as a matter of course because the scene here can change quite dramatically over the space of half an hour.

Resident and breeding species hold more than a passing interest, as a walk around the perimeter of the farm and its fields will soon prove. **Firecrest** are common as are **Turtle Doves** and **Spanish Crossbills.** The latter, which are less brightly coloured than our own native crossbill, are easily located for they are often at the water cistern near the track at the back of the farm where they perch on the filler-pipe to take a drink. Walking away from the farm and water cistern, at the second right-angled bend in the track, there is a path leading off up the hillside where the scrub contains a healthy population of **Scrub-warblers** and where a little searching may pay dividends in the form of a **Marmora's.** **Dartford Warblers** are scarce winter visitors on Mallorca but I have one reliable breeding record from this area, which is in fact the only nest of this species I have heard of. Looking back over the trees may give a glimpse of the scarce **Woodpigeon** or, more likely, a **Booted Eagle.**

## Cabo Formentor

The continuation of the road from Casas Veyas leads further through the mountains towards the lighthouse at Cabo Formentor. Shortly before the final stretch, the road passes through a short tunnel and it is possible to park at the viewpoint on the left to take in the view of the small bay at Cala Figuera. This area is also of particular interest to the botanist as several of the more unusual plants can be seen here. **Red-legged Partridges** are frequently seen along the next stretch of road and **Blue Rock Thrushes** are common. The power lines crossing the road are worth a second look as I have more than once seen a **Roller** perched in full view here. The viewpoints along the road to the lighthouse offer spectacular views of the rugged coastline of the peninsula.

Continue to the end of the road and park in the lighthouse car park. The car park wall runs right along the cliff edge where **Cory's** and **Balearic Shearwaters** are almost certain to be seen flying over the sea below. At this distance it is still quite easy to differentiate between them; the smaller balearics have a rapid flickering wingbeat compared to the more lugubrious almost slow flight of the cory's, both spend a lot of time gliding on rigid wings. By leaving the car park and walking around to the back of the lighthouse, the more adventurous visitors can find their way down through the wood below the lighthouse onto an area of open, flat rocks which provide a much closer vantage point from which to observe the seabirds. The woods also provide cover for resting migrants. The car park itself is a good spot to see **Hirundines** and **Swifts**. **Crag Martins** are resident but it takes quite a bit of perseverance to pick out the rarer **Red-rumped Swallow** or **Pallid Swift** from amongst their common relatives. The low wall just around the first bend in the road below the car park is the best place to watch for **Eleonoras Falcons;** particularly in late summer and autumn when they are feeding their young in nests in the cliff face opposite. They live in an uneasy peace with the resident **Peregrines** and aerial battles are not infrequent. I witnessed one, between three Eleonoras and one Peregrine, which carried on for over 10 minutes far out to sea in the general direction of Minorca. It can be a bit of an effort to have to leave, when food or the fleshpots of Puerto Pollensa call, but the consolation is that one can always stop off for a few minutes at Casas Veyas on the way back

## GENERAL

The Hotel Formentor is situated near to the junction of the left turn for Cabo Formentor. It has a nice beach and a bar and restaurant which is open to non-residents. A regular boat sails from Puerto Pollensa directly to the beach and is a convenient way to visit Casas Veyas which is only a short, pleasant walk along the road through the woods.

# Cuber and the Mountain Habitats

LOCATION
In the north, between Soller and Pollensa.

ACCESS (See map p.47)
From Puerto Pollensa via the Pollensa road, keep to the right when reaching Pollensa Town (left-hand branch of main road is signposted Inca/Palma) and carry straight on. After a long straight, running through the farmlands, the road starts to climb rapidly and twists and turns in a series of hairpin bends. The road leads right the way along the northern mountain chain passing all the birdwatching sites mentioned below. If spending the day at Cuber, retracing the route back to Pollensa is the shortest way back.

For those with an extra couple of hours to spare, a more circuitous return route is available via Bunyola, Orient and Alaro. To take this route, carry onto Soller and turn left on the main road towards Palma; a series of 50 or so hairpin bends takes you 17 kilometres/10.5 miles over the mountains to where the road straightens out. Bunyola is on the left but care must be taken not to overshoot the turn-off. After turning keep to the left on entering the town and turn left up the narrow road marked Orient. The next 20 kilometres/12.5 miles of road runs along the valley through Orient and emerges at Alaro from where you can follow the signs back to the Inca/Palma road and from thence return to Pollensa.

HABITAT
Mountain rock and scree, balearic zone, sea cliffs, pine and oak forest, maquis and garigue scrub, freshwater lakes and a small reed bed at Cuber.

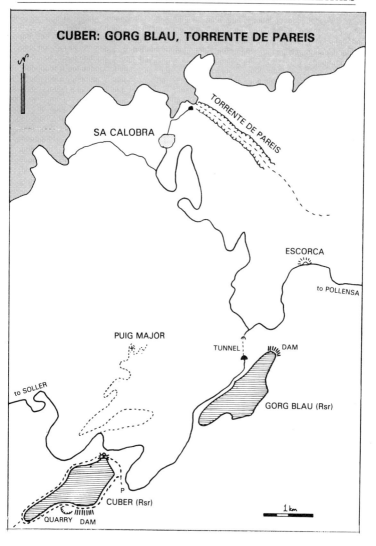

**CUBER: GORG BLAU, TORRENTE DE PAREIS**

SA CALOBRA

TORRENTE DE PAREIS

ESCORCA

to POLLENSA

PUIG MAJOR

TUNNEL

DAM

GORG BLAU (Rsr)

to SOLLER

P

CUBER (Rsr)

QUARRY  DAM

1 km

BIRDS

K8

The popular stopping place at the K8 kilometre post, once re-
nowned for views of **Red Kites** and **Black Vultures,** is now no
better than anywhere else along the road as the rubbish tip which
attracted the birds has been closed.

## Manut

Situated near the K17 marker post, the recreation area at Manut
is a suitable stopping place to explore the oak woods. **Blue Tits,**
seldom seen in more lowland areas except in winter, frequent
these woods as do summer visiting and migrant **Warblers**. I have
twice seen a **Goshawk** over the picnic site, my only personal
records of this species on the island. They are reputed to have bred
here but, as migrant raptors commonly migrate following the
mountain chain, this may be a coincidence. Further detailed
reports of sightings would be appreciated.

## Lluch

Built between the 17th and 18th centuries, the monastery at
Lluch is reached via the well signposted minor road on the right
about a mile past Manut. The monastery is sited in a scenically
beautiful valley which holds a good selection of woodland and
farmland birds like **Cirl** and **Corn Buntings, Willow Warblers**
and **Nightingales.** Many birds of prey, including the resident
**Booted Eagles,** pass overhead and there is always the chance of
a **Black Vulture.** Paths lead from the monastery into the surrounding area.

## Escorca

Further along the main road you will come to a T-junction
signposted Inca to the left and Soller to the right. Turn right
towards Soller and continue to the next point of interest at Escorca
where you will find a viewpoint in the form of a low semi-circular
wall on the right-hand side of the road. Take care to park off the

BEE ORCHID

SWALLOWTAIL

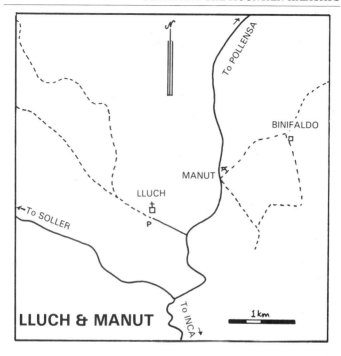

**LLUCH & MANUT**

highway. The viewpoint offers stunning views of the surrounding mountain crags; the deep cleft visible in the mid-distance is the Torrente de Pareis (see below). This is an excellent spot from which to see passing raptors, like **Ospreys** commuting to and from Cuber or migrating **Harriers**, and the open aspect allows sightings of approaching **Black Vultures** from miles away. It is well worth spending at least half an hour here on the off-chance that a B.V. will turn up; while you're waiting you should get excellent close-up views of the local **Crag Martins** - both above and below. This is also the spot where I got my one and only Mallorcan close-up look at a **Bonelli's Eagle.**

## Torrente de Pareis and La Calobra

Continuing from the viewpoint towards Soller you will see a minor road on the right signposted Sa Calobra. The road down is extremely tortuous and it is better attempted first thing in the morning before the coaches arrive as it is impossible to overtake and very frustrating to get stuck behind one. Parking in the small town can also get quite chaotic when the coaches arrive. The small road which you pass on the left is worth investigating on the return journey as the gardens, citrus and olive groves often harbour small falls of migrants. The Torrente itself is reached through a pedestrian tunnel through the rock which emerges at what is, in spring and early summer, a quite sizeable lagoon of water trapped behind the shingle ridge of the beach. Unless you are prepared to swim or wade, this prevents further access up the stream bed. However, later in summer the lagoon dries out and it is possible to walk up. The sheer walls rise to over 500 feet and at times are only yards apart. The route is very arduous and is not recommended for the inexperienced; proper footwear must be worn. The route may also be attempted in the other direction from the small Chapel of Sant Pere near the viewpoint at Escorca (see above), but the downward route is no less severe. Birds of the Torrente include **Blue Rock Thrush, Crag Martin** and **Alpine Swift.**

Between May and September boat trips operate to Soller from Sa Calobra harbour. This is an ideal way to see the fantastic cliffs of the northern coast, whilst keeping a look out for **Shearwaters** on the sea and **Raptors** and **Rock Doves** along the crags.

## Gorg Blau and Cuber

Just past the Sa Calobra turn-off, the road starts to rise and passes through a short tunnel through the mountainside. The tunnel emerges at the Gorg Blau Reservoir which is named after the deep blue of the water it contains. This lake is very steep sided and deep and does not attract the quantity or variety of birds to be found just a few kilometres up the road at Cuber, so I usually give it a quick scan from the roadside and press on.

The reservoir at Cuber is one of the best birdwatching spots on the island and it is well worth spending the best part of a day here at least once during a holiday. Try and pick a day when the weather is good as it can get quite cool this high up. The small car park is at the bend where you first see the lake and access is gained through a gate. The path leads down towards the lake and branches left and right almost immediately. For no other reason than personal preference, I usually begin my circumnavigation of the lake by keeping to the left. Use the binoculars to check the tops of the power pylons on the far side of the lake as these are a favourite perch for the resident **Ospreys**. The path levels out and heads for the dam. The stony area on the right is a good spot for **Tawny Pipits** and **Short-toed Larks,** whereas the scrub on the right is one of the few breeding places for **Spectacled Warblers.** It is not necessary to leave the path and disturb the birds to get a glimpse of them as just before the dam there are a couple of large block-like rocks which they frequently use as a perch.

I recommend taking lunch by the dam as this is a great spot to sit and await developments. The area below the dam is constantly visited by numerous species coming to drink at the small stream and pools there. **Ospreys** fish in the reservoir and sometimes come almost within touching distance, oblivious of human presence, and the area is part of the territory of the **Rock Thrushes** which have bred in the small quarry just over the dam for the past few years. This species is a very scarce breeder on Mallorca, unlike its close relative the **Blue Rock Thrush** which is common throughout the mountains.

If the **Rock Thrushes** have not put in an appearance you can check out the quarry after lunch. The lakeside below is a favourite bathing place for **Ospreys** and **Eleonoras Falcon.** The path drops down a little, passing an area of hillside on the left which is a likely spot for **Red-legged Partridges,** shortly before crossing the stream bed to turn right and come back along the other side of the lake. This area is also good for **Tawny Pipits**. The path becomes an embankment which provides good overviews of the scrub on the left. I have regularly seen **Sub-alpine Warblers** in this area and suspect that they may have bred here. The point where the pylons leave the embankment and start to ascend the ridge is an ideal place to stop and wait for a photograph of an **Osprey**, as they favour this route when returning to the eyrie with fish and pass directly overhead at close range in an east to west direction. There is also a better than average chance of seeing a **Red Kite** somewhere along the route.

Shortly after crossing the concrete feeder-channel there are some small, scattered holm oaks which are usually frequented by **Cirl Buntings**; I have located up to five calling males in this one small area. It is also the point where I saw a **Pine Marten** taking prey to her kittens. The walk is nearly complete here, except for a short investigation of the postage stamp-sized reed bed in the stream on the right before returning to the car park.

The cwm above the car park is a favoured spot for **Black Vultures**, notwithstanding that a weather-eye should be kept out throughout any visit as they can appear from nowhere. The past few years has seen a vagrant **Griffon Vulture** keeping company with them.

**Orient and Alaro** (See ACCESS p.46)
The road from Bunyola winds and climbs through woodland bordered by steep mountains before dropping down into the small, fertile valley around Orient. This is, to my mind, one of the most scenic pastoral spots on the island, doubtless preserved by the fact that coaches cannot gain access through the narrow streets of Bunyola. The woods harbour resident **Firecrests**, **Blue** and **Great Tits**, and many summer visitors like **Spotted Flycatchers**, **Nightingales** and **Turtle Doves**. The farmlands see the passage of migrant passerines and hold **Corn** and **Cirl Buntings**, **Woodchat Shrikes** and **Goldfinches**. In spring, flocks of **Bee-eaters** move through, often only located by their 'Quip - Quip' call note as they pass high overhead. Another sound which may be heard at this time is the repetitive 'Kew-kew-kew-kew' call of **Wrynecks**

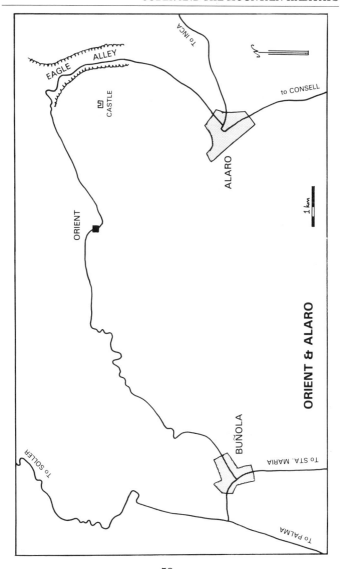

skulking in the trees.

This is good **Booted Eagle** country as they often come down off the crags into the farmland. If **Booted Eagles** have proved elusive elsewhere you might like to try 'Eagle Alley'. This is past Orient where the road bends right at Sollerich and passes along one side of a gorge flanked by almost vertical mountainsides. I have christened it 'Eagle Alley' because the birds regularly pass through between the cliffs and good eye-level views can be had. I should mention that pale phased birds outnumber the dark phase by about three to one, but reports of sightings by visitors tend to be almost the reverse. I can only put this down to female **Marsh Harriers** being well and truly confused with dark phased **Booted Eagles**, as **Harriers** on passage are frequently seen along the mountain chain as well as both passage and resident birds being seen in the more normal habitat around the marshes.

GENERAL

### Puig Major
The buildings on the summit are part of the NATO early warning system and the area is controlled by the military which prevents access to the island's highest point.

### Lluch Monastery
Besides two restaurants, the monastery has a museum which contains artifacts of the prehistoric peoples of Mallorca.

# Albuferetta and Nightingale Road

LOCATION
North-west of the island between Alcudia and Puerto Pollensa.

ACCESS (See maps p.30 &59)
From Puerto Pollensa/Alcudia coast road take the metalled road signposted Pollensa near C'an Guarassa Restaurant. The route around the marsh covers a distance of about 11 kilometres/7 miles and can be undertaken on foot or by bicycle.

HABITAT
Minor roads cross the arable farmland dotted with many olive and citrus groves. Part of the route runs alongside a tamarix-lined stream which feeds into the freshwater marsh/reed bed.

BIRDS
The farmland and tamarix scrub at the start of the route is interesting for migrants in the spring and **Sardinian Warblers, Fan-tailed Warblers** and **Corn Buntings** breed here. The drier areas are often visited by **Short-toed Larks** and, following a period of easterly winds in April/May, the power lines crossing the fields are a favourite perch for **Red-footed Falcons.**

After approximately 2.5 kilometres/1.5 miles turn left at a right-hand bend marked with chevrons and follow the road, which I have nicknamed Nightingale Road, bordering the stream on the left. The tamarix along the stream often shelters roosting **Night Herons** and many species come to the water to drink. Carry on around a sharp right bend, passing the small rustic-looking electricity sub-station, and take the rough road on the left until you see the umbrella-like skeleton of a wind pump on the right. Park on the flat area on the left and walk on 50 metres past the second farm outbuilding to the rough track on the left which leads down to a gate at the marsh edge. The past few years have seen migrating **Cattle Egrets** with the cows in this boggy area and the trees at the back should be carefully scanned for roosting **Herons** and **Egrets. Grey, Purple, Squacco** and **Night Herons** and **Little Egrets** have all been present at the same time. **Frogs,** of course, abound and it is possible to catch a fleeting glimpse of a **Grass-snake** crossing the path.

Returning to the road continue 1 kilometre for a view overlooking fields and the marsh on the left. Migrating **Marsh Harriers** add to the numbers of resident birds and **Quail** can be heard calling from the crops - sometimes from almost beneath your feet, but they are only likely to be glimpsed crossing one of the paths or at the edge of a newly cut area. Carrying straight on will bring you out on the Alcudia/Palma road about 150 metres west of the Puerto Pollensa road. Turn left to return along the Puerto Pollensa road to the minor road on the left alongside a bar with a '7 Up' sign - just along here you can overlook the lake on the edge of the marsh. **Red-throated Pipits** are among the scarcer migrants which have been seen in the fields here and the **'Spanish' Wagtail** is a common breeder. Between here and Puerto Pollensa the road crosses a small river which enters the sea across the beach on the right. This mini-estuary attracts **Kentish Plovers, Black-winged Stilts** and various other waders on passage. **Squacco Herons** are fairly regular visitors to the channel edges of the inland side and **Audouin's Gull** has turned up on the beach side. The best views of the marsh can be obtained by taking the rough road which filters to the left at the bridge and turning left along the first track. The flat, rocky area near the stand of pine trees provides a good viewpoint and also boasts a good population of **Mirror** and **Serapia Orchids** in spring. Besides the almost inevitable **Marsh Harriers, Montagu's Harriers** are regular passage visitors here too.

The aforementioned C'an Guarrassa Restaurant also has a noteworthy attraction. The small road at the side of the restaurant leads a short distance through the coastal tamarix to a spot where **Red-footed Falcons** habitually turn up in small numbers in spring. East winds are the best but a small detour here each time you are passing will often provide good views of them sitting on the power lines. I have no idea what the attraction of this particular corner is, but they definitely seem to favour it and usually hang around for a week or so. My best total to date is 12.

## GENERAL
The tracks leading from the road to the marsh all cross private land and discretion should be employed before using them. In particular, please do not enter closed gates. This is one of the places where it pays to have a chat with the local farmers and check that you are not trespassing. If the track is not gated or leading to a private house it is most unusual for permission to be refused.

Little Egret

# Albufera and Old Salinas

LOCATION
North-west of the island, between Alcudia and Ca'n Picafort

ACCESS (See maps p.30 &59)
From Alcudia continue along the main coast road towards Ca'n Picafort, the marsh is on the right-hand side.

## Orange Bridge
Passing the Sa Pobla turn-off, turn into the slip road in front of the shops and then right at the end of the last building. The bridge, which is a good place to overlook the power station infills, is now painted green but the name has stuck.

## Albufera Reserve Visitor Centre
Further along the coast road you will pass the Esperanza Hotel on the left before crossing the English bridge. The reserve entrance is on the right, immediately after crossing the main drainage canal. The access road leads into the marsh and there are toilets and a car park at the visitors centre.

## The Old Salinas
These extend from the campsite on the north side of Ca'n Picafort back towards Alcudia between K24 and K25 on the coast road. Park off the road under the trees. Most of the salt pans can be viewed from the roadside.

HABITAT
The reserve itself is mainly a vast reed bed with drainage channels and tamarix and willow shrub. The power station land consists of shallow lagoons with embankments and some areas of sedge and

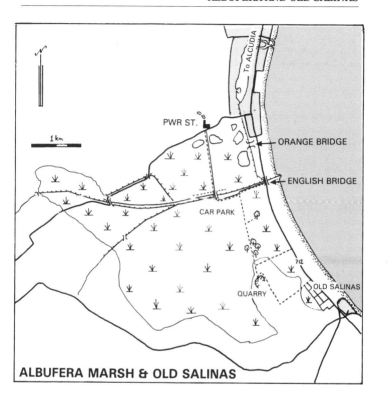

mud flats. The old salinas are disused salt pans with varying depths of shallow water crossed by raised banks and bordered on one side by the coastal pine belt and on the other by reeds.

## BIRDS

The marsh and its adjacent areas are, beyond doubt, the most important site for birdwatchers in the whole of the Balearics. It is almost impossible for me to describe adequately all of its many attractions (which include flora and fauna as well as birds). A visit to the Albufera from Puerto Pollensa normally starts with a call at Orange Bridge and works down to the old salinas.

## Orange Bridge

Morning is the best time to visit the bridge as the sun is behind the observer and the birds are not just silhouettes. The gate across the bridge is usually locked. **Note:** Even if it is open it is unwise to enter as you would be likely to find it locked against you when you return. The bridge provides an excellent vantage point from which to overlook the pools on the far side of the canal. A visit here on a good day in spring can delay any further progress until well into the afternoon. **Purple Herons** and **Kentish Plovers** breed here, as do **'Spanish' Wagtails.** You are certain to have the whole of your stay punctuated by the calls of **Fan-tailed Warblers** which are everywhere and they really live up to their other name of **Zitting Cisticola** as they continually fly in an udulating circuit calling incessantly 'Zit-zit-zit'. The pools play host to many water birds - migrant waders like **Greenshank, Spotted Redshank, Stints** and even the occsional small party of **Avocets. Whisk-ered Terns** are regulars and other **Marsh Terns (Gull-billed, Black** and **White-winged Black)** all pay fleeting calls. Added interest may come in the form of an irregular **Slender-billed** or **Common Gull,** or even a rare **Common Tern.** Most of the wildfowl like **Ferruginous Duck, Pochard** and **Tufted Duck,** are winter visitors, but **Shoveler** and **Garganey** often stay late and can  be seen well into spring. Birds of prey include both resident and migrant **Osprey** and **Marsh Harriers** which can be expected to turn up in an hour or so, weather permitting. **Eleonoras Falcons** arrive here in spring and sometimes appear in squadron strength of a dozen or more swooping low over the observer's head to catch airborne insects. **Hen-harriers** and **Montagu's Harriers** are less regular, but there is more than a fair chance of seeing the spectacular stoop of a **Peregrine** as it scatters all before it in complete disarray. Less regular visitors to the lagoons include **Great White Egrets, Spoonbills** and **Greater Flamingoes.**

**Visitor Centre and Public Hides**

The road entering the reserve initially runs between the main channel and a minor channel. The trees isolated by the water on the left of the entrance are a favourite roosting place for **Night Herons** which are best seen at sunset when they fly out to feed on the marsh. I have seen as many as 14 take to the air in succession. However birds have a habit of doing the unexpected: one particularly amusing incident occurred one evening when around 20 birdwatchers were scanning the skies and all the birds walked across the access road, unnoticed by most, before disappearing in the reeds at the edge of the main channel!

Around the car park there are trees and scrub where **Woodchat Shrikes** often take post and **Blackcaps, Whitethroats** and **Nightingales** are also to be found.

The track to the first of the hides starts at the top of the car park at the visitor centre. **Bee Orchids** can be found growing conveniently next to the signpost for the hide. The path leads into the marsh and crosses one of the channels via a wooden bridge. The hide - called the Watkinson Hide - overlooks one of the smaller channels and an artificially cleared section of the marsh with a small pool. The perches and posts provided attract passing **Harriers** and **Ospreys**, which never seem to stay for long, and the holes in the banks of the channel are the homes of the introduced **Freshwater Crayfish** which sometimes oblige by emerging in the open. Resident species include **Cettis, Moustached Warblers** and the local race of **Reed Bunting** which is larger than our own. Visiting waders can be seen here but not in the variety or number which are to be found at the other hide or the old salt pans. The largest **Grass-snake** I have ever seen - over six feet long - was spotted basking in the sun at the side of the path as I returned over the bridge one day.

Returning, take the wooden bridge where the path bends back towards the car park, then follow the path past the buildings on the right to cross the first of three small stone bridges. It is well worth stopping for a while at the first bridge as patience is often rewarded by the appearance of a **Little Bittern.** These birds are commoner here than most people think; in 1986 British ringers caught five different **Little Bitterns** in one 50 metre stretch of net in a week. They spend most of their time deep in the reeds and are usually only seen briefly as they fly along or across one of the channels before diving into cover again. The channel leading into the marsh away from this bridge is probably about the best spot for seeing one, but perseverance is needed. However, time spent here is rarely wasted, even when not occupied with the local **Reed, Great-reed, Cetti's, Moustached** or even **Savis Warblers,** the passage of **Hirundines** can run into thousands per hour. Close examination of this passage may result in a bonus of a **Red-rumped Swallow.**

The third stone bridge leads onto the rough road that crosses the marsh towards the power station as well as the path to the Watkinson Hide. At the far end of the bridge, on the left-hand side, a small spring emerges immediately next to the stonework. This spring attracts small fish which, in turn, attract the **Viperine Snakes** which are almost certain to be found there, basking in the spring sunlight on the stones. Being cold-blooded, they do not often emerge until the warmer weather has arrived. The two hides, down the path on the right between the bridges, give excellent views over the edge of the power station marsh. The number of species recorded from here is far too great to mention in detail but there is always something going on. **Purple Herons** and **Little Egrets** stand out among the sedge; waders like **Wood, Marsh** and **Green Sandpipers** stop in passing to feed on the muddy margins in front of the hide; **Marsh Harriers** pass close by and, sometimes, a wintering or passage migrant **Kingfisher** uses the roof as a perch. This is also the area where **Spotted Crakes** are most likely to put in a 10-second appearance (which is 9 seconds longer than most).

The road to the power station separates the sedge marsh from the reed beds proper. A hot and dusty walk on a warm day, yet it is well worth taking, at least as far as the point where the power station pools open out on each side. These pools usually attract a good selection of waders like **Greenshank, Spotted Redshank, Redshank** and **Little** or even **Temminck's Stints. Little Grebes** breed here and the area on the right seems to be attractive to the irregular **Collared Pratincoles** which seem more likely to turn up after a few days of east winds in late spring. The wall at the side of the road provides food and shelter for **Wall Geckos** which vanish from view at the slightest incautious movement, a response, no doubt, which helps them avoid becoming a **Hoopoe's** dinner. One other inhabitant of the marsh which is quite common in this section is the **European Pond Tortoise** (*Emys orbicularis*) which are also nervous of approach but can often be seen at the water's edge on sunny days.

Access to the third hide is via the track which runs on into the marsh from between the two bridges. It is a tall, metal construction without seats. Of little use for birdwatching (flying **Marsh Harriers** and the like excepted) it does, however, give a panoramic view of the extent of the reserve. The steel spiral staircase lends itself to entanglement with tripods and these are better left at the bottom.

## Ses Puntes Path

A short distance back along the access road between the car park and the coast, where the road bends sharply left and then right, another path leads off to the right. Both sides of the track are frequented by **Moustached** and **Cetti's Warblers** and the pig-like squeals of **Water Rails** are constantly heard. The fig tree on the right is a favourite perch of **Woodchat Shrikes** while 'Spanish' **Wagtails** breed in the scrubby areas of the marsh. If orchids are of interest, the small wood further along the main path is one of the best places to see them. Although at their best earlier in the year for species like **Sawfly Orchids**, the ground beneath the trees is still covered in **Bee, Marsh** and **Pyramidal Orchids** in April and early May in such profusion that great care is needed in avoiding treading on them. It can be difficult to find a clear patch in which to sit and examine them more closely. Both **Bog** and **Bumblebee Orchids** also occur.

## The Old Salinas
This is one of the best sites on the whole island for really good views of migrant waders and other waterbirds. The shallow salt pans are flooded by winter rains and gradually dry out in the summer. What is particularly good is that the water is deeper at the Ca'n Picafort end and gets progressively shallower toward Alcudia. Different depths attract different species, the encroachment of reeds and sedge to the pools and scrub on the embankments providing additional habitat. The comparatively small area covered by this site belies its almost magnetic attraction for birds and gives the added bonus that they can be observed from close range. The best views are obtained from the roadside banks. Please give consideration to other birdwatchers by not entering other areas or disturbing the birds. Special care is needed not to disturb nesting birds like **Black-winged Stilt** which breed on the fringes of the more overgrown areas.

Residents and summer visitors include **Cetti's, Sardinian, Great Reed, Reed, Moustached** and **Fan-tailed Warblers, Purple Heron** and **Little Bittern, Black-winged Stilt, Common Sandpiper, Kentish** and **Little Ringed Plovers, Coot Moorhen** and **Water Rail.**

RISTART (female)

TAWNY PIPIT

Spring brings a bountiful supply of passage migrants. Among the commoner waders are **Lapwing, Dunlin, Ringed Plover, Common** and **Temminck's Stints, Green, Wood** and **Curlew Sandpipers, Spotted Redshank, Redshank, Ruff** and **Greenshank** - all of which can be recorded in a single visit. **Little Egret, Squacco Heron, Whiskered, Little, White-winged Black** and **Black Terns** are other regular visitors. Scarcer species include the **Gull-billed Tern, Grey Plover, Avocet, Knot, Collared Pratincole, Common** and **Little Gulls.**

## Son Boch

Take the rough road at the northern end of the old salt pans and turn right at the end of the reed beds. The sand quarry here has been re-colonised by **Bee-eaters** which are present from the end of April until August. There are usually several unworked faces for them to build their distinctive arch-shaped burrows in. **Bee-eaters** have had a pretty torrid time of things on Mallorca with many colonies being destroyed by development. For some time it was feared that they had lost the battle to stay as a breeding species. This colony is now thriving with more than 50 pairs present. They are very easy to observe and even photograph as they perch on nearby favourite shrubs and power lines. The area is just outside the Albufera Reserve and you can be of real assistance by *not* entering the colony whilst breeding is in progress. **Stone Curlews** have been reported from the fields around here and **Barn Owls** hunt over the rougher areas, including the banks of the sandworks, and the locally common **Brown Rat** probably features in their diet. I once found a barn owl here which had been shot, but this kind of occurrence is fortunately rare. The sandworks road is chained off to vehicles but access can be had on foot by skirting the edge of the sandworks to the right. Following the path through Ses Puntes Farm you can enter the reserve along the path through the orchid wood to the car park - remembering to obtain a visitors permit from the reserve office (see below).

The **Night Heron** roost near the English Bridge is quite near;

the more nocturnally minded visitor could easily make a combined post-dusk visit here. Even if a **Barn Owl** doesn't show up, the asdic-like calls of the common **Scops Owls** declare their own presence.

## GENERAL

The Albufera Reserve covering a total area of 4,000 acres, has a justifiable prominence as one of Europe's most important wetlands. It has, in the not too distant past, been under severe threat from being lost to development. Part of the marsh, near the Hotel Esperanza, has been built on and this was only the thin end of the wedge which would have seen the destruction of the whole area. Due to local pressure from the G.O.B. (the Balearic Ornithologists' Club), aided in no small part by British birdwatchers and residents, the cause was adopted by the Spanish Government's Nature Conservancy Body (ICONA) and the marsh is now fully protected as a nature reserve. It is fitting that one of the leading lights of this campaign, the late Eddie Watkinson, is commemorated in the name of the first hide to be built on the reserve.

The reserve now boasts an excellent visitor centre, with car parking and toilet facilities and has public hides from which to view the birds.

**Note:** Visitors must obtain a permit to visit the reserve on the day of their visit. These are available from 9.00 a.m. onwards at the visitor centre. At present there is no charge but permits must be obtained for each separate day's visit. Wardens are present at all times and you should not enter the reserve before 9.00 a.m.

# Arta Mountains

LOCATION
North-east of Manacor.

ACCESS (See map p.68)
Telecom Tower
Enter Arta Town via the Alcudia/Arta road, which becomes progressively narrower and walled-in by buildings, until reaching a T-junction. Turn right and take the second narrow road on the left, signposted 'Ermita de Betlem'. Skirt the left-hand edge of the church and follow the road taking the first fork on the left, signposted 'Ermita'. Just over 3 kilometres further on, fork right where the sign to the left is for the 'Ermita'. The road winds on upwards for 6 or 7 kilometres, passing through two sets of rough gates* before reaching the telecommunications tower compound. Due to the narrow roads in Arta the route is inaccessible to coaches.

**Lower Road and Club Naval**
Between the K9 and K10 markers on the Alcudia/Arta road, take the minor road signposted 'Colonia San Pere', keep to the right when approaching the village and continue straight on to Betlem. Once past the roundabout the Club Naval is well signposted to the left. To complete the journey continue straight on until the road deteriorates into a rough, open area where you can park.

---

*The gates may be closed to prevent livestock wandering, please ensure that you close and secure them behind you. Recently the gates have been padlocked on occasions. If this happens return to the junction, follow the route for the Ermita for about 7 kilometres/4.25 miles and park at the crest of the ridge overlooking the sea - descending the other side will only restrict the view.

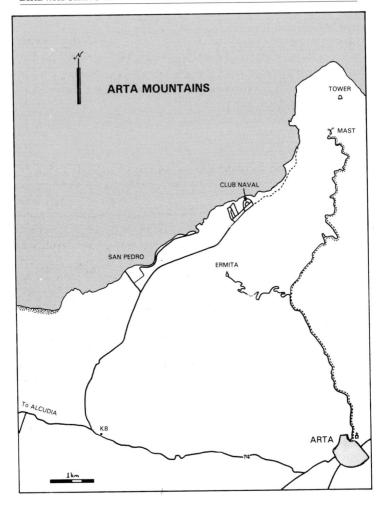

## HABITAT

Although called mountains, the Artas are in fact a range of hills with the highest (Morey) only 561 metres high. The higher terrain consist of steep crags, wooded slopes ascending to dry garigue with palmetto and amplodesmus grass. Lower areas consist of farmland and coastal scrub.

## BIRDS

### Telecom Tower

Immediately on the right when leaving the town, the church here was at one time publicised as a possible site for seeing **Lesser Kestrel.** This, alas, seems to be no longer the case; in fact I have not heard of any reliable reports of this species from anywhere on the island for at least the last five years - any fully detailed records would be appreciated. The **Booted Eages** are still here, although in reduced numbers, and generally manage to turn up. The main draw to the area for most birders is the elusive **Thekla Lark,** which does occur elsewhere but is extremely local. The area immediately around the tower compound is the best bet as, not only do the larks definitely breed here, but it also gives excellent views over the surrounding countryside and can be a stopping off place for migrants like **Wheatears. Booted Eagles** often come within close range and seem to favour the area around Atalaya de Morey which forms the headland to the north. **Red-legged Partridges** are common and are most likely to be seen around the last 2 kilometres of the road to the tower.

The alternative route to the Ermita ridge does not guarantee **Thekla Larks** but provides an open aspect from which to watch for **Booted Eagles.**

The Artas are also irregularly visited by **Black Vultures** and **Egyptian Vultures** straying from the northern mountains.

## Lower Road and Club Naval

This area typifies the need for the 'one eye on the pot and the other up the chimney' technique required at so many of the places covered by this book. **Marmora's Warblers** frequent the scrub, along with many migrants among the commoner **Sardinian Warblers.** The fortunate few may even turn up the scarcer migrating varants like **Orphaean, Melodious** or **Icterine Warblers** in the shrubbery. The 'other eye' must scan the crags for passing **Booted Eagles** or summer visiting **Alpine Swifts** among the resident **Ravens** (which often oblige by rising to the occasion and escorting passing raptors off their patch).

Lunch either before or after birdwatching can be taken at the Club Nautico (Club Naval) where the food is excellent and non-diners can, for the price of a drink, take a dip in the swimming pool or lounge in the sun while watching the cliffs for passing eagles. The locally rare and very striking **Cardinal Butterfly** may be seen feeding on the ornamental flowering shrubs of the club in the late summer.

Bonelli's Eagle

# Porto Colom

LOCATION
South-east coast between Cala D'or and Porto Christo.

ACCESS (See map p.72)
From Manacor via Felanitx take the left turning to follow the sign for Porto Colom. Continue as signposted, turning right at the Santany/Porto Christo road and finally left to the town itself. On reaching the waterfront follow one of the two routes detailed below.

HABITAT
Marine harbour, open fields, scrub, low coastal cliffs.

BIRDS
Pride of place of all the birds which occur here must go to the **Audouin's Gull.** Keep the harbour on the left on entering the town, pass the first small pier which is for pleasure craft and walk along the second which is for commercial vessels. If not already in evidence, the gulls can usually be enticed into putting in an appearance by the simple expedient of throwing bread onto the water. At such close range it is easy to distinguish even the juveniles, with their characteristic wing pattern, from the more numerous **Herring Gulls.**

To reach the lighthouse and headland, turn left at the waterfront and follow the road through the town, noting the minor road on the left at the second sharp right. **Cory's** and **Balearic Shearwaters** are usually present off-shore and it is the best spot to try for the **Audouin's Gulls** if they are absent from the harbour. Summer visiting **Pallid Swifts** breed on the cliffs around the headland; their paler colour is much easier to see when

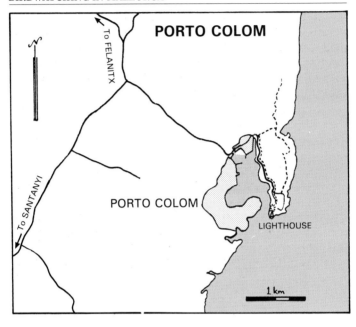

viewed from above against the sea in the background.

Return to the minor road mentioned above. The road leads past fields on the left and the rock and scrub of the headland on the right. It is well worth devoting some time to this area looking for **Red-legged Partridges, Stone Curlews, Thekla** and **Short-toed Larks** in the fields; **Marmora's Warblers** in the scrub. Lunch on the top of the low cliffs, to the right of the small bay at the end of the metalled part of the road, is a relaxing way to keep an eye out for the **Pallid Swifts.** The benefits of sitting in one spot for a while were more than proved to me when taking lunch here one day. My attention was attracted to a large bird out at sea which at first seemed like a flamingo flying low over the water - neck outstretched in typical fashion. As it approached, I saw it was a **Great White Egret** struggling to reach landfall, head straining forwards and wings brushing the surface, until finally it reached land and climbed gratefully to safety on the thermal over the rock. A very rare vagrant to the island, the bird flew off inland and, as far as I know, was not seen by any other birdwatcher. An isolated record, but very pleasing.

# Salinas de Campos and Cabo Salinas

LOCATION
South, between Campos del Puerto and Ses Salines.

ACCESS (See map p.75)

## Salinas

From Lluchmayor or Felanitx, on entering Campos follow the signs for Santany to the right turn signposted 'Colonia San Jordi'. The salinas (salt pans) are on the right-hand side about 7 kilometres further on at the start of the minor road to Es Trenc which starts alongside the works buildings. Additional viewpoints are along various roads and tracks from the Banos de San Juan end of the salinas, lead off the Colonia San Jordi road around the Sa Barrala area.

## Cabo Salinas

From Campos via Ses Salines or from Felanitx via Santany; then from the Ses Salines/Santany road turning south down Cabo Salinas road.

HABITAT
Open working salt pans, derelict salt pans, reeds, embankments, open scrub, coastal pine woods, farmland.

BIRDS

## Salinas

The management of the salines used to allow free access to the embankments but this is now, sadly, no longer the case. Due to various disputes, some unfortunately due to the behaviour of

74

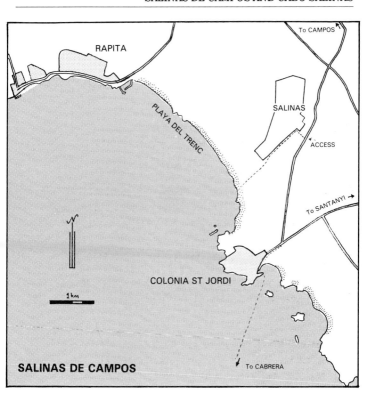

irresponsible birdwatchers, the main access is restriced to a small path at the southern end which leads to the coast. Plenty of birds can still be seen from the roadside, although a telescope is a must for scanning the furthest pans.

In summer, **Black-winged Stilts** are everywhere, **Kentish Plovers** and **Little Ringed Plovers** also occur in sizeable numbers. Spring means the passage of waders and terns. More than 20 species of migrant waders are commonly recorded including **Ringed Plover, Little Stint, Black-tailed Godwit, Purple** and **Marsh Sandpipers. Avocets** are more regular visitors here than on the other sites on the island, as are **Whiskered, Black** and **White-winged Black Terns. Gull-billed Terns** seem to be turning up more regularly than in the past. The salinas cover a fairly extensive area which acts as a magnet to birds making their first landfall since Africa. There is a constantly changing pattern of new arrivals, departures and frequent movement between the lagoons. Because of this, most time and attention should be paid to this area where patience is nearly always rewarded. Remarkably, for British birdwatchers, **Knot, Sanderling, Common** and **Sandwich Tern** are among the less-common visitors and an **Oystercatcher** is a five-star bird. I blithely added one to my list one day as I drove past, only to find out later that it was the first seen on the island for several years, which made me revise my ideas on what constitutes a 'rare' bird.

The small, overgrown sand quarry on the left, just past the works buildings is periodically used as a nesting site by a few pairs of **Bee-eaters.** The surrounding open shrub and rough ground are good for many species; **Short-toed Lark, Fan-tailed Warbler,** and **'Spanish' Wagtail** all breed, while 'falls' of commoner migrants sometimes include irregular visitors like **Black-eared Wheatears** or **Ortolan Buntings. Resident Stone Curlews** can be difficult to locate and are seen more frequently during the earlier part of the morning or around dusk; they may also be seen from the road leading to Colonia San Jordi.

The path to the beach at Es Trenc wanders through the coastal pinewoods. Although the **Bee-eater** colonies along the coast (which were the island's last stronghold for the species and made the walk an essential part of any visit) have been lost to the bulldozer, the ever-present **Serins** and **Firecrests** associate with numerous migrants.

## Cabo Salinas

The land on either side of the road near the Cape is one of the best places to see the **Stone Curlew,** particularly earlier in the day, and a search may be rewarded with **Thekla Larks.**

The Cape itself is a good sea-watch viewpoint. Migrant **Black** and **Gull-billed Terns** pass in numbers and both **Cory's** and **Ballearic Shearwaters** come close in-shore on suitable winds. **Audouin's Gulls** are reasonably certain at any time.

GENERAL

For those staying in and around Pollensa and Alcudia, the trip down to the salinas occupies a full day and is only really worth-while if spending more than a week on the island as the nearer habitats are more than enough to fill 7 days.

# Cabrera

LOCATION
Island group 9 kilometres south-west of southern tip of Mallorca.

ACCESS (See map p.79)
By boat from Colonia San Jordi (route as Salinas de Campos see
p.74). Pleasure cruises run throughout the summer season from
mid-May onwards, depending on the weather, but landings are by
military permit only.

HABITAT
Rocky off-shore marine islands, coastal cliffs, scrub.

BIRDS
Cabrera (pron. Cab-ray-ra) is the largest island of the group of 20
or so isles and islets. Approximately 2 miles square and rising to
a height of some 100 metres it is far larger than Conejera, the next
in size at 125 hectares/half a square mile.

Owned by King Juan Carlos, Cabrera is at present occupied by
the Spanish army, landings are by military permit only and
visitors are restricted to within 30 metres of the sea. This is for a
good reason as even the military don't know where all the unex-
ploded shells are! This may make it sound a pretty unprepossess-
ing sort of place, but it has many attractions for the birdwatcher/
naturalist. The passage to the island by fishing boat takes about
an hour. These boats are of open construction and about 10 metres
long. The passengers sit on the foredeck hatchcovers whilst the
skipper steers from the covered cockpit and the crewman perches
unconcernedly on the side with the sea passing about a foot
beneath him - tempting providence.

The nearest of the group is Foradada with its sentinel light-

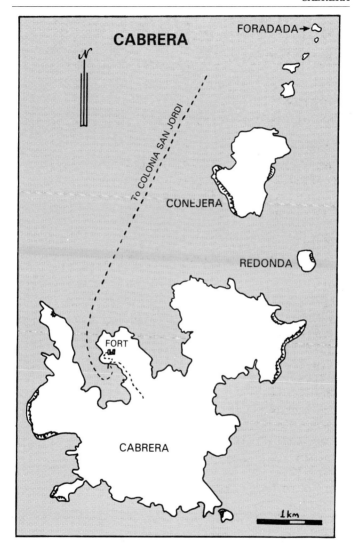

house warning larger ships off. Rafts of **Shearwaters,** both of the **Balearic** race of the **Manx Shearwater** and the large, more languorous **Cory's** with its yellow bill, which are usually to be found in this spot, sometimes come within 10 metres of the boat. This apparent fearlessness reflects the healthy respect that the local fishermen have for them, treating them as familiar friends, unlike some of their land-living counterparts who have a penchant for shooting anything that moves. The seabirds usefulness in indicating the presence of fish and squid gives them a better image which no doubt aids this relationship. The boat then skirts the island of Conejera with its large colony of **Shags** standing soldier-like around cliffs topped by the similarly erect giant **Spurges** *(Euphorbia characias).* The shags themselves are distinctly larger than the British version and are of the Mediterranean race *(Phalacrocorax aristotelis desmarestii).* Half a mile to the south-east of Conejera lies the islet of Redonda which has a breeding colony of **Audouin's Gulls** among the local yellow-legged **Herring Gulls;** a little bread cast on the water brings them close enough to the boat for their tri-coloured bills to show up well. Fortunately this rare and attractive gull is now well established and thriving in its various Balearic colonies.

For those parties which have permission to land, lunch is usually accompanied, literally, by another of Cabreras' specialities - **Lilfords Wall Lizard** *(Podarcis lilfordi kuligae),* a melanistic island race with a surprisingly kingfisher-blue underside. These lizards can be enticed to emerge from the scrub to eat scraps of fruit which are placed down for them. One particularly bold individual once climbed into my jacket pocket to look for more!

For several years now the island has boasted a breeding pair of **Ospreys** whose cliff nest is nearly 2 metres high and columnar - not pyramidical as one would expect - the sides rising vertically from the broad ledge on which it is placed. Its situation is so perfectly sheltered from the gales that the accumulated additions of the years has stood firm.

The turning point for the return journey is Punta Anciola, the

SUB ALPINE WARBLER

MARSH FROG

cape which bears the lighthouse marking the south-west corner of the group. **Peregrine Falcons** breed on the cliffs here and are often seen zooming along the cliff edge driving some of the resident **Shags** to plunge for shelter beneath the waves. This side of the island is still bordered by cliffs which extend north-west in three promontories which enclose two bays. The first, like a small fjord, contains Puerto Cabrera - the wharf which serves the garrison stationed in the shadow of the very impressive-looking small fortress perched on the cliff above. This area is the only part of the island which was previously farmed, now under the control of the army its citrus and olive groves are a haven for birds on passage, but off-limits. Provided permission to land has been obtained, visitors, usually accompanied by a soldier, can investigate the castle and its surrounding scrub with a good chance of seeing **Marmora's** or even **Dartford Warblers** providing the wind is light.

The once experienced, never forgotten 'cantina' provides a welcome cool beer before time demands a return to the boat, this time to sail the final leg to the mainland. You pass once more through the rafts of **Shearwaters;** spring may bring **Black** or **Gull-billed Terns** to join them in crossing the wake of the boat.

## GENERAL

One of the sea caves on the south side of Cabrera was the last western Mediterranean breeding place of the **Monk Seal** *(Monachus monachus)* which is still maintaining a tenuous foothold around Greece and Turkey. The small remaining numbers of eastern seals are considered a pest by fishermen and are also threatened by tourist development of the sandy beaches which they prefer to frequent. I am led to believe that, should conservation efforts be successful there, there may be an attempt to re-establish the western population and Cabrera seems to be a suitable starting point.

A piece of good news. The military are rumoured to be relinquishing possession of the islands in the near future and the group may become a Nature Reserve. At present, landing being restricted, the wildlife is only being disturbed by howitzers and hand-grenades, to which it seems reasonably indifferent. The true value of the area as first landfall for tired migrants can only be imagined.

Green Sandpiper

# San Telmo

LOCATION
North-west of Andraitx, overlooking Dragonera.

ACCESS (See map p.84)
Leave Andraitx via the S'Arraco road and follow the signs for San Telmo. On reaching the town continue along the coast road towards the far side of town (signs for Punt Blanc). Where the road bends right follow signs for La Trappa to the car park opposite the farmhouse of Cala Den Basset.

HABITAT
Headland, pinewood, mountain crags and scree.

BIRDS
By following the signs for 'La Trappa' (the monastery), the path passes through woodlands before emerging onto more open slopes and the remainder of a stiff 1,200 foot climb. The lower route to the Torre is less strenuous and still excellent for many of the birds. **Migrant Warblers, Firecrests, Serins** and **Scops Owls** are the denizens of the woods. The owls are abundant but are almost impossible to locate during the day. However, if you are able to locate one, despite the camouflage, they are extremely approachable. On a warm day, a slow wander through the woodland, particularly after a hard climb, provides a reasonable excuse to cool off in the shade while adding to the day's list of birds.

The north-west end of the mountain chain still has a few resident **Red Kite** and (although I have not heard of any current reports), if **Bonelli's Eagles** are still on the island this is the most likely place for them to be seen. The higher areas are also where one is likely to discover **Alpine Swifts.**

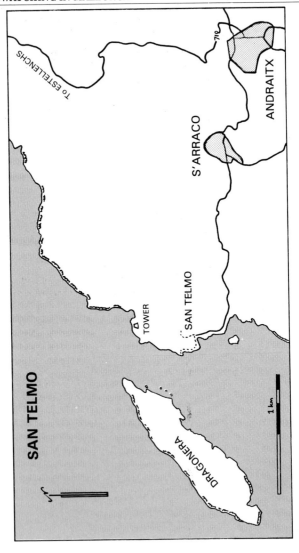

Before returning through the village, a small diversion to the right along the headland is recommended. The headland overlooks the channel between Mallorca and Dragonera. **Ballearic Shags** are certain to be in evidence. **Audouin's Gulls** are a distinct possibility and Dragonera's resident **Ospreys** may well turn up.

If there is time to spare, the return drive from Andraitx can be via the road south of the mountains, through Capdella, Puigpunent and Esporlas. This is a very scenic and tortuous route, but a few stops at suitable vistas along the way may bear fruit with a glimpse of one of the scarcer **Raptors.**

GENERAL

Much of the area is a G.O.B. ((Balearic Ornithologists' Club) reserve. Information leaflets are available but, as yet, only in Mallorquin.

For those motoring from the east of the island, Andraitx is best reached via the Alcudia/Palma route as the drive along the tortuous and constricted mountain road, whilst scenic, can take more than 3 hours each way.

# Special Species

Everywhere has its own 'special' bird, on Mallorca there is no doubt that the **Black Vulture** attracts most attention (appropriately they are the logo of the Balearic Ornithologists' Club, the G.O.B.). Affectionately known by visiting birdwatchers as B.V.s, their massive size and 9 foot wing-span can only be described as awesome as they glide among the peaks of the northern Sierras. Their passage from skyline to skyline, without a single wingbeat, is amazingly rapid, as is their ability to rise on a thermal until only a speck in the sky. The short head and tail give an almost all-wing silhouette, from which their less complementary nickname of 'the flying plank' arises.

The **Vultures** breed on the sea cliffs in November and are, naturally, more active around this time. Although stated as 30/50 birds in *The Handbook of Birds of the Western Palearctic,* there has been a steady decline in their numbers through persecution and reduction of food sources. Current estimates of population are 15/20 individuals with only occasional records of successful breeding. Great efforts are now being made to preserve the birds and enhance their image as an emblem of the island.

The value of records of some of the scarcer or threatened species cannot be overstated in assisting in their conservation and protection. The increasing awareness of the precious heritage which an area's wildlife represents is exemplified by the current progress being made in Spain in general and on Mallorca in particular. One only has to look at recent television wildlife documentaries: the quality of production is very high and, more to the point, their popularity with the Spanish people themselves highlights the move towards environmental consciousness.

I have little doubt that the Spanish Government, through ICONA (the Spanish Nature Conservancy Body), is well to the fore of all the Mediterranean countries in its efforts to preserve their natural assets, both for the benefit of their own people and as a tourist resource. On Mallorca this is underpinned by the contribution of voluntary organisations like the G.O.B. whose membership is growing rapidly and reflects this increased interest. It is also very encouraging to see a tremendous willingness to accept help and advice from their friends. The work of British bird-ringers from the B.T.O., the presence of an R.S.P.B. representative and the information received from visiting birdwatchers, entomologists and botanists have all contributed to the national record.

It is very easy to paint an overly rosy picture, the current situation is genuinely hopeful but there are still many problems to solve. The amount of time spent in the field by visiting enthusiasts represents a valuable source of information which can help fill the gaps in records of many species which are scarce or underrecorded. I would be interested to receive any records of the following species from anyone who would like to help.

## INSECTS

| | |
|---|---|
| Scarce Swallowtail* | *Iphiclides podalirius* |
| Camberwell Beauty* | *Nymphali antiopa* |
| Cardinal | *Pandoriana pandora* |
| Southern Gatekeeper* | *Pyronia cecilia* |

## REPTILES

| | |
|---|---|
| Cowl Snake* | *Macroprotodon cucullatus* |
| Ladder Snake* | *Elaphe scalaris* |
| Land Tortoise | *Testudo hermanni* |

## BIRDS

| | | |
|---|---|---|
| Storm Petrel | *Hydrobates pelagicus* | |
| Squacco Heron | *Adeola raloides* | (Summer only [b?]) |
| Cattle Egret | *Bubulcus ibis* | *(Summer only [b?])* |
| Great White Egret | *Egrett alba* | |
| Garganey | *Anas querquedula* | (Summer only [b?]) |

| | | |
|---|---|---|
| Red Kite | *Milvus milvus* | (other than Cuber) |
| Goshawk* | *Accipiter gentilis* | |
| Bonelli's Eagle* | *Hieraaetus pennatus* | |
| Lesser Kestrel* | *Falco biarmicus* | |
| Spotted Crake* | *Porzana porzana* | |
| Baillon's Crake* | *Porzana pusilla* | |
| Stone Curlew | *Burhinus oedicnemus* | |
| Barn Owl | *Tyto alba* | |
| Tawny Owl | *Stryx aluco* | |
| Nightjar | *Caprimulgus europaeus* | |
| Alpine Swift | *Apus melba* | |
| Thekla Lark | *Galerida theklae* | (other than Puig Tudosa) |
| Blue Rock Thrush | *Monticola solitarius* | (other than Cuber) |
| Dartford Warbler* | *Sylvia undulata* | |
| Spectacled Warbler* | *S. conspicillata* | (Summer only [b?] other than Cuber |
| Sub-alpine Warbler | *S. cantillans* | (Summer only[b?]) |
| Rock Sparrow* | *Petronia petronia* | |

MAMMALS

| | |
|---|---|
| Wild Cat* | *Felis sylvestris* |
| Pine Marten | *Martes martes* |
| Gennet* | *Genetta genetta* |

Where possible, records should include exact location as well as date, time, weather conditions and details of sighting. Sightings of species marked * should include a full description. Records may be sent to me (see Addresses).

**Note:** Reports of illegal shooting, trapping etc. should be made immediately to the G.O.B. (see Addresses).

# Bibliography

*Birds of the Western Palearctic: Handbook of the Birds of Europe, the Middle East and North Africa.*   Oxford 1977 onwards.

*Birds of Britain and Europe* - Heinzel, Fitter & Parslow.   Collins 1972

*A Field Guide to the Birds of Britain & Europe* - Peterson Mountfort & Hollom.   Collins 1954

*Flight Identification of European Raptors* - Porter, Willis, Christensen & Neilsen.   Poyser 1974

*A Guide to Birdwatching in Mallorca* - Watkinson   Sanders 1979

*The Naturalist in Majorca* - Parrack.   David & Charles 1973

*Butterflies of Britain & Europe* - Higgins & Hargreaves.   Collins 1983

*Plants of the Balearic Islands* - A. Bonner      Editorial Moll, Mallorca 1983

*Walking In Mallorca* - J. Parker    Cicerone 1986

By the same author
*Birdwatching on Merseyside* - K.J. Stoba    Cicerone 1989

## Addresses

The Author
  Ken Stoba, 16 Hadfield Grove,
  Liverpool, L25 8RR.
  Tel: 051-428-2350
  (Please send s.a.e. if writing.)

G.O.B.    (Balearic Ornithologists' Club
  Grupo Ornithologia Balear,
  Calle Veri 1-3° 2a Palma.

Spanish Tourist Board
  57 St. James Street,
  London SW1.

R.S.P.B./ GOB Representative,
  Grahame Hearl,
  Aptdo. De Correas 83
  Sa Pobla,
  Mallorca

# Bird Check List

Principal Status:
R=Resident, W=Winter visitor, S=Summer visitor, M=Migrant, A=Annual vagrant, V=Vagrant.

| SPECIES | STATUS | MON | TUES | WED | THURS | FRI | SAT | SUN | MON | TUES | WED | THURS | FRI | SAT | SUN | TOTAL |
|---|---|---|---|---|---|---|---|---|---|---|---|---|---|---|---|---|
| Red-throated Diver | V | | | | | | | | | | | | | | | |
| Black-throated Diver | V | | | | | | | | | | | | | | | |
| Great Northern Diver | V | | | | | | | | | | | | | | | |
| Little Grebe | R | ✓ | | | | | | | | | | | | | | |
| Great Crested Grebe | V | | | | | | | | | | | | | | | |
| Black-necked Grebe | W | | | | | | | | | | | | | | | |
| Red-necked Grebe | V | | | | | | | | | | | | | | | |
| Slavonian Grebe | V | | | | | | | | | | | | | | | |
| Cory's Shearwater | R | | | | | | | | | | | | | | | |
| Manx Shearwater | M | | | | | | | | | | | | | | | |
| Ballearic Shearwater | R | | | | | | | | | | | | | | | |
| Storm Petrel | R | | | | | | | | | | | | | | | |
| Leaches Petrel | V | | | | | | | | | | | | | | | |
| Gannet | A | | | | | | | | | | | | | | | |
| Cormorant | W | ✓ | ✓ | | | | | | | | | | | | | |
| Shag | R | ✓ | | | | | | | | | | | | | | |
| Bittern | V | | | | | | | | | | | | | | | |
| Little Bittern | S | | | | | | | | | | | | | | | |
| Night Heron | M | ✓ | ✓ | | | | | | | | | | | | | |
| Little Egret | R | ✓ | ✓ | | | | | | | | | | | | | |
| Cattle Egret | W | ✓ | ✓ | | | | | | | | | | | | | |
| Squacco Heron | S | ✓ | ✓ | | | | | | | | | | | | | |
| Great White Heron | V | | | | | | | | | | | | | | | |
| Grey Heron | W | ✓ | ✓ | | | | | | | | | | | | | |
| Purple Heron | R | ✓ | ✓ | | | | | | | | | | | | | |
| Spoonbill | V | | | | | | | | | | | | | | | |
| Black Stork | V | ✓ | | | | | | | | | | | | | | |
| White Stork | A | | | | | | | | | | | | | | | |
| Glossy Ibis | V | | | | | | | | | | | | | | | |
| Greater Flamingo | M | ✓ | | | | | | | | | | | | | | |
| Greylag Goose | A | | | | | | | | | | | | | | | |
| Bean Goose | V | | | | | | | | | | | | | | | |
| Whooper Swan | V | | | | | | | | | | | | | | | |
| Shelduck | V | | | | | | | | | | | | | | | |
| Wigeon | W | | | | | | | | | | | | | | | |

| | | M | T | W | T | F | S | S | M | T | W | T | F | S | S | Total |
|---|---|---|---|---|---|---|---|---|---|---|---|---|---|---|---|---|
| Teal | W | | | | | | | | | | | | | | | |
| Mallard | R | ✓ | | | | | | | | | | | | | | |
| Pintail | W | | | | | | | | | | | | | | | |
| Gadwall | V | | | | | | | | | | | | | | | |
| Garganey | W | ✓ | | | | | | | | | | | | | | |
| Shoveler | W | ✓ | | | | | | | | | | | | | | |
| Marbled Teal | V | | | | | | | | | | | | | | | |
| Pochard | W | ✓ | ✓ | | | | | | | | | | | | | |
| Ferruginous Duck | W | | | | | | | | | | | | | | | |
| Tufted Duck | W | ✓ | | | | | | | | | | | | | | |
| Red-breasted Merganser | V | | | | | | | | | | | | | | | |
| Goosander | V | | | | | | | | | | | | | | | |
| Osprey | R | ✓ | ✓ | | | | | | | | | | | | | |
| Honey Buzzard | M | ✓ | | | | | | | | | | | | | | |
| Black Kite | M | ✓ | | | | | | | | | | | | | | |
| Red Kite | R | ✓ | ✓ | | | | | | | | | | | | | |
| Egyptian Vulture | A | ✓ | | | | | | | | | | | | | | |
| Black Vulture | R | ✓ | ✓ | | | | | | | | | | | | | |
| Gryffon Vulture | A | ✓ | | | | | | | | | | | | | | |
| Short-toed Eagle | M | | | | | | | | | | | | | | | |
| Marsh Harrier | R | ✓ | ✓ | | | | | | | | | | | | | |
| Hen-harrier | A | ✓ | | | | | | | | | | | | | | |
| Pallid Harrier | V | | | | | | | | | | | | | | | |
| Montagu's Harrier | M | | | | | | | | | | | | | | | |
| Goshawk | R | | | | | | | | | | | | | | | |
| Sparrowhawk | M | | | | | | | | | | | | | | | |
| Buzzard | M | ✓ | | | | | | | | | | | | | | |
| Golden Eagle | A | | | | | | | | | | | | | | | |
| Booted Eagle | R | ✓ | | | | | | | | | | | | | | |
| Bonelli's Eagle | V | | | | | | | | | | | | | | | |
| Lesser Kestrel | V | | | | | | | | | | | | | | | |
| Kestrel | R | ✓ | ✓ | | | | | | | | | | | | | |
| Red-footed Falcon | M | ✓ | | | | | | | | | | | | | | |
| Merlin | V | | | | | | | | | | | | | | | |
| Hobby | A | | | | | | | | | | | | | | | |
| Eleonoras Falcon | S | ✓ | ✓ | | | | | | | | | | | | | |
| Lanner Falcon | V | | | | | | | | | | | | | | | |
| Saker Falcon | V | | | | | | | | | | | | | | | |
| Peregrine | R | ✓ | ✓ | | | | | | | | | | | | | |
| Red-legged Partridge | R | | | | | | | | | | | | | | | |
| Quail | S | | | | | | | | | | | | | | | |

# BIRDWATCHING IN MALLORCA

| | | M | T | W | T | F | S | S | M | T | W | T | F | S | S | Total |
|---|---|---|---|---|---|---|---|---|---|---|---|---|---|---|---|---|
| Crane | A | | | | | | | | | | | | | | | |
| Water Rail | R | | | | | | | | | | | | | | | |
| Spotted Crake | R | | | | | | | | | | | | | | | |
| Little Crake | V | | | | | | | | | | | | | | | |
| Baillon's Crake | V | | | | | | | | | | | | | | | |
| Corncrake | V | | | | | | | | | | | | | | | |
| Moorhen | R | ✓ | ✓ | | | | | | | | | | | | | |
| Coot | R | ✓ | ✓ | | | | | | | | | | | | | |
| Little Bustard | V | | | | | | | | | | | | | | | |
| Oystercatcher | V | ✓ | | | | | | | | | | | | | | |
| Black-winged Stilt | S | ✓ | ✓ | | | | | | | | | | | | | |
| Avocet | M | | | | | | | | | | | | | | | |
| Stone Curlew | R | | | | | | | | | | | | | | | |
| Collared Pratincole | A | | | | | | | | | | | | | | | |
| Little Ringed Plover | R | ✓ | ✓ | | | | | | | | | | | | | |
| Ringed Plover | M | ✓ | ✓ | | | | | | | | | | | | | |
| Kentish Plover | R | ✓ | ✓ | | | | | | | | | | | | | |
| Dotterel | V | | | | | | | | | | | | | | | |
| Golden Plover | M | | | | | | | | | | | | | | | |
| Grey Plover | A | ✓ | | | | | | | | | | | | | | |
| Lapwing | W | | | | | | | | | | | | | | | |
| Knot | A | | | | | | | | | | | | | | | |
| Sanderling | A | | | | | | | | | | | | | | | |
| Little Stint | M | ✓ | ✓ | | | | | | | | | | | | | |
| Temminck's Stint | A | | | | | | | | | | | | | | | |
| Curlew Sandpiper | M | ✓ | | | | | | | | | | | | | | |
| Dunlin | M | | | | | | | | | | | | | | | |
| Ruff | M | ✓ | | | | | | | | | | | | | | |
| Jack Snipe | V | | | | | | | | | | | | | | | |
| Snipe | W | ✓ | ✓ | | | | | | | | | | | | | |
| Woodcock | W | | | | | | | | | | | | | | | |
| Black-tailed Godwit | M | | | | | | | | | | | | | | | |
| Bar-tailed Godwit | A | | | | | | | | | | | | | | | |
| Whimbrel | V | | | | | | | | | | | | | | | |
| Slender-billed Curlew | V | | | | | | | | | | | | | | | |
| Curlew | W | | | | | | | | | | | | | | | |
| Spotted Redshank | M | | | | | | | | | | | | | | | |
| Redshank | R | ✓ | ✓ | | | | | | | | | | | | | |
| Marsh Sandpiper | A | | | | | | | | | | | | | | | |
| Greenshank | M | ✓ | | | | | | | | | | | | | | |
| Green Sandpiper | W | | | | | | | | | | | | | | | |

| | | M | T | W | T | F | S | S | M | T | W | T | F | S | S | Total |
|---|---|---|---|---|---|---|---|---|---|---|---|---|---|---|---|---|
| Wood Sandpiper | M | ✓ | ✓ | | | | | | | | | | | | | |
| Common Sandpiper | W | ✓ | ✓ | | | | | | | | | | | | | |
| Turnstone | A | | | | | | | | | | | | | | | |
| Red-necked Phalarope | V | | | | | | | | | | | | | | | |
| Grey Phalarope | V | | | | | | | | | | | | | | | |
| Great Skua | V | | | | | | | | | | | | | | | |
| Mediterranean Gull | A | | ✓ | | | | | | | | | | | | | |
| Little Gull | M | | | | | | | | | | | | | | | |
| Black-headed Gull | W | ✓ | ✓ | | | | | | | | | | | | | |
| Slender-billed Gull | A | ✓ | | | | | | | | | | | | | | |
| Aoudouin's Gull | R | ✓ | ✓ | | | | | | | | | | | | | |
| Common Gull | V | | | | | | | | | | | | | | | |
| Lesser Black-backed Gull | A | ✓ | | | | | | | | | | | | | | |
| Herring Gull | R | | ✓ | | | | | | | | | | | | | |
| Greater Black-backed Gull | V | | | | | | | | | | | | | | | |
| Kittiwake | V | | | | | | | | | | | | | | | |
| Gull-billed Tern | M | ✓ | | | | | | | | | | | | | | |
| Caspian Tern | V | | | | | | | | | | | | | | | |
| Sandwich Tern | A | | ✓ | | | | | | | | | | | | | |
| Common Tern | V | | | | | | | | | | | | | | | |
| Little Tern | M | | | | | | | | | | | | | | | |
| Whiskered Tern | M | ✓ | | | | | | | | | | | | | | |
| Black Tern | M | ✓ | | | | | | | | | | | | | | |
| White-winged Black Tern | M | ✓ | | | | | | | | | | | | | | |
| Razorbill | A | | | | | | | | | | | | | | | |
| Puffin | V | | | | | | | | | | | | | | | |
| Rock Dove | R | ✓ | | | | | | | | | | | | | | |
| Stock Dove | V | | | | | | | | | | | | | | | |
| Woodpigeon | R | ✓ | ✓ | | | | | | | | | | | | | |
| Collared Dove | V | | | | | | | | | | | | | | | |
| Turtle Dove | S | ✓ | | | | | | | | | | | | | | |
| Great Spotted Cuckoo | V | | | | | | | | | | | | | | | |
| Cuckoo | M | ✓ | | | | | | | | | | | | | | |
| Barn Owl | R | | | | | | | | | | | | | | | |
| Scops Owl | R | ✓ | | | | | | | | | | | | | | |
| Little Owl | V | | | | | | | | | | | | | | | |
| Tawny Owl | R | | | | | | | | | | | | | | | |
| Long-eared Owl | V | | | | | | | | | | | | | | | |
| Short-eared Owl | V | | | | | | | | | | | | | | | |
| Nightjar | M | | | | | | | | | | | | | | | |
| Swift | S | ✓ | ✓ | | | | | | | | | | | | | |

| | | M | T | W | T | F | S | S | M | T | W | T | F | S | S | Total |
|---|---|---|---|---|---|---|---|---|---|---|---|---|---|---|---|---|
| Palid Swift | S ✓ | | | | | | | | | | | | | | | |
| Alpine Swift | S | | | | | | | | | | | | | | | |
| Kingfisher | W | | | | | | | | | | | | | | | |
| Bee-eater | S ✓ | | | | | | | | | | | | | | | |
| Roller | A | | | | | | | | | | | | | | | |
| Hoopoe | R ✓ | ✓ | | | | | | | | | | | | | | |
| Wryneck | S | ✓ | | | | | | | | | | | | | | |
| Calandra Lark | V | | | | | | | | | | | | | | | |
| Short-toed Lark | S ✓ | ✓ | | | | | | | | | | | | | | |
| Lesser Short-toed Lark | V | | | | | | | | | | | | | | | |
| Crested Lark | V | | | | | | | | | | | | | | | |
| Thekla Lark | R | | | | | | | | | | | | | | | |
| Woodlark | V | | | | | | | | | | | | | | | |
| Skylark | V | | | | | | | | | | | | | | | |
| Sand Martin | M ✓ | ✓ | | | | | | | | | | | | | | |
| Crag Martin | R ✓ | ✓ | | | | | | | | | | | | | | |
| Swallow | S ✓ | ✓ | | | | | | | | | | | | | | |
| Red-rumped Swallow | M ✓ | | | | | | | | | | | | | | | |
| House Martin | S ✓ | ✓ | | | | | | | | | | | | | | |
| Tawny Pipit | S ✓ | ✓ | | | | | | | | | | | | | | |
| Tree Pipit | M ✓ | | | | | | | | | | | | | | | |
| Meadow Pipit | M | | | | | | | | | | | | | | | |
| Red-throated Pipit | A | | | | | | | | | | | | | | | |
| Water/Rock Pipit | V | | | | | | | | | | | | | | | |
| Yellow Wagtail | M ✓ | ✓ | | | | | | | | | | | | | | |
| Iberian Wagtail | S | | | | | | | | | | | | | | | |
| Blue-headed Wagtail | M | ✓ | | | | | | | | | | | | | | |
| Grey-headed Wagtail | M | | | | | | | | | | | | | | | |
| Ashy-headed Wagtail | M | | | | | | | | | | | | | | | |
| Black-headed Wagtail | V | | | | | | | | | | | | | | | |
| Grey Wagtail | W | | | | | | | | | | | | | | | |
| Pied/White Wagtail | W ✓ | ✓ | | | | | | | | | | | | | | |
| Wren | R ✓ | ✓ | | | | | | | | | | | | | | |
| Dunnock | W | ✓ | | | | | | | | | | | | | | |
| Alpine Accentor | W | | | | | | | | | | | | | | | |
| Rufous Bush Chat | A | | | | | | | | | | | | | | | |
| Robin | W | | | | | | | | | | | | | | | |
| Nightingale | S ✓ | | | | | | | | | | | | | | | |
| Bluethroat | A | | | | | | | | | | | | | | | |
| Black Redstart | W ✓ | ✓ | | | | | | | | | | | | | | |
| Redstart | M ✓ | ✓ | | | | | | | | | | | | | | |

| | | M | T | W | T | F | S | S | M | T | W | T | F | S | S | Total |
|---|---|---|---|---|---|---|---|---|---|---|---|---|---|---|---|---|
| Whinchat | M | | | | | | | | | | | | | | | |
| Stonechat | R | ✓ | ✓ | | | | | | | | | | | | | |
| Wheatear | M | ✓ | | | | | | | | | | | | | | |
| Black-eared Wheatear | A | ✓ | ✓ | | | | | | | | | | | | | |
| Blackbird | R | ✓ | ✓ | | | | | | | | | | | | | |
| Fieldfare | W | | | | | | | | | | | | | | | |
| Song Thrush | W | ✓ | | | | | | | | | | | | | | |
| Redwing | W | | | | | | | | | | | | | | | |
| Mistle Thrush | W | | | | | | | | | | | | | | | |
| Golden Oriole | M | ✓ | | | | | | | | | | | | | | |
| Rock Thrush | S | ✓ | ✓ | | | | | | | | | | | | | |
| Blue Rock Thrush | R | ✓ | | | | | | | | | | | | | | |
| Cetti's Warbler | R | ✓ | ✓ | | | | | | | | | | | | | |
| Fan-tailed Warbler | R | ✓ | ✓ | | | | | | | | | | | | | |
| Grasshopper Warbler | V | | | | | | | | | | | | | | | |
| Savi's Warbler | S | | | | | | | | | | | | | | | |
| Moustached Warbler | R | ✓ | ✓ | | | | | | | | | | | | | |
| Aquatic Warbler | V | | | | | | | | | | | | | | | |
| Sedge Warbler | M | | | | | | | | | | | | | | | |
| Reed Warbler | S | | | | | | | | | | | | | | | |
| Great Reed Warbler | S | ✓ | ✓ | | | | | | | | | | | | | |
| Oliveaceous Warbler | V | | | | | | | | | | | | | | | |
| Icterine Warbler | A | | | | | | | | | | | | | | | |
| Mellodious Warbler | A | | | | | | | | | | | | | | | |
| Sardinian Warbler | R | ✓ | ✓ | | | | | | | | | | | | | |
| Marmora's Warbler | R | ✓ | | | | | | | | | | | | | | |
| Dartford Warbler | W | | | | | | | | | | | | | | | |
| Spectacled Warbler | S | ✓ | | | | | | | | | | | | | | |
| Sub-Alpine Warbler | M | | | | | | | | | | | | | | | |
| Orphean Warbler | V | | | | | | | | | | | | | | | |
| Lesser-Whitethroat | V | | | | | | | | | | | | | | | |
| Whitethroat | M | ✓ | ✓ | | | | | | | | | | | | | |
| Garden Warbler | M | ✓ | | | | | | | | | | | | | | |
| Blackcap | R | ✓ | ✓ | | | | | | | | | | | | | |
| Pallas Warbler | V | | | | | | | | | | | | | | | |
| Bonelli's Warbler | M | | | | | | | | | | | | | | | |
| Wood Warbler | M | ✓ | | | | | | | | | | | | | | |
| Chiff-chaff | M | ✓ | | | | | | | | | | | | | | |
| Willow Warbler | M | ✓ | | | | | | | | | | | | | | |
| Goldcrest | M | | | | | | | | | | | | | | | |
| Firecrest | R | ✓ | | | | | | | | | | | | | | |

| | | M | T | W | T | F | S | S | M | T | W | T | F | S | S | Total |
|---|---|---|---|---|---|---|---|---|---|---|---|---|---|---|---|---|
| Spotted Flycatcher | S | | | | | | | | | | | | | | | |
| Red-breasted Flycatcher | V | | | | | | | | | | | | | | | |
| Semi-collared Flycatcher | V | | | | | | | | | | | | | | | |
| Collared Flycatcher | A | | | | | | | | | | | | | | | |
| Pied Flycatcher | M | | | | | | | | | | | | | | | |
| Blue Tit | R | | | | | | | | | | | | | | | |
| Great Tit | R | | | | | | | | | | | | | | | |
| Penduline Tit | W | | | | | | | | | | | | | | | |
| Short-toed Treecreeper | V | | | | | | | | | | | | | | | |
| Red-backed Shrike | V | | | | | | | | | | | | | | | |
| Lesser Grey Shrike | V | | | | | | | | | | | | | | | |
| Great Grey Shrike | V | | | | | | | | | | | | | | | |
| Woodchat Shrike | S | | | | | | | | | | | | | | | |
| Alpine Chough | V | | | | | | | | | | | | | | | |
| Chough | V | | | | | | | | | | | | | | | |
| Rook | V | | | | | | | | | | | | | | | |
| Carrion/Hooded Crow | A | | | | | | | | | | | | | | | |
| Raven | R | | | | | | | | | | | | | | | |
| Starling | W | | | | | | | | | | | | | | | |
| Spotless Starling | V | | | | | | | | | | | | | | | |
| House Sparrow | R | | | | | | | | | | | | | | | |
| Tree Sparrow | V | | | | | | | | | | | | | | | |
| Rock Sparrow | R | | | | | | | | | | | | | | | |
| Snowfinch | V | | | | | | | | | | | | | | | |
| Chaffinch | R | | | | | | | | | | | | | | | |
| Brambling | V | | | | | | | | | | | | | | | |
| Serin | R | | | | | | | | | | | | | | | |
| Citril Finch | V | | | | | | | | | | | | | | | |
| Greenfinch | R | | | | | | | | | | | | | | | |
| Goldfinch | R | | | | | | | | | | | | | | | |
| Siskin | W | | | | | | | | | | | | | | | |
| Linnet | R | | | | | | | | | | | | | | | |
| Spanish Crossbill | R | | | | | | | | | | | | | | | |
| Hawfinch | V | | | | | | | | | | | | | | | |
| Snow Bunting | V | | | | | | | | | | | | | | | |
| Yellowhammer | V | | | | | | | | | | | | | | | |
| Cirl Bunting | R | | | | | | | | | | | | | | | |
| Rock Bunting | V | | | | | | | | | | | | | | | |
| Ortolan Bunting | M | | | | | | | | | | | | | | | |
| Little Bunting | V | | | | | | | | | | | | | | | |
| Reed Bunting | R | | | | | | | | | | | | | | | |
| Corn Bunting | R | | | | | | | | | | | | | | | |